AGAINST THE FLOW STUDY GUIDE

Discussing and applying the message of
Daniel today

John C. Lennox
Joseph McRae Mellichamp

First published in Great Britain in 2024

SPCK

SPCK Group
Studio 101
The Record Hall
16–16A Baldwin's Gardens
London EC1N 7RJ

www.spck.org.uk

British Library Cataloguing-in-Publication Data
A catalogue record for this book is available from the British Library

ISBN 978-0-281-08924-6
eBook ISBN 978-0-281-08925-3

1 3 5 7 9 10 8 6 4 2

Typeset by
Manila Typesetting Company

First printed in Great Britain by Clays Limited

eBook by Manila Typesetting Company

Produced on paper from sustainable sources

John C. Lennox MA PhD DPhil DSc FISSR is Emeritus Professor of Mathematics at the University of Oxford and Emeritus Fellow in Mathematics and the Philosophy of Science at Green Templeton College. He is also a Fellow of the International Society for Science and Religion on which topic he has lectured at many prestigious institutions around the world. He has publicly debated Richard Dawkins and Christopher Hitchens, among others. He is also the author of many books including *Cosmic Chemistry: Do God and science mix?*; *Can Science Explain Everything?*; *Friend of God: Discussing and applying the message of Abraham today* and *Stephen Hawking: Whose design is it anyway?*

Joseph McRae Mellichamp is Emeritus Professor of Management Science at the University of Alabama. In addition to academic research, he has published study guides for several important books, including *Mere Christianity, The Man in the Mirror* and *The Training of the Twelve*. He and his wife Peggy have spoken at more than 150 universities and colleges and made more than 35 international ministry trips in their work with the Faculty Ministry of CRU, which they helped to set up in the 1970s and 1980s.

Contents

Contents

Foreword

About 2,600 years ago Nebuchadnezzar, the king of Babylon, invaded Jerusalem and deported many of the Jews from their homes in Jerusalem and the surrounding area to Babylon, where they would remain as captives for many years. Four of these prisoners we know as Daniel, Hananiah, Mishael and Azariah, and Daniel tells us in his personal account that they were captured as young men, probably in their teens. Their experiences, documented for us in the biblical book of Daniel, represent some of the most thrilling stories in the Bible: the four men in the fiery furnace, the handwriting on the wall, and Daniel in the lions' den. Many of us were excited to hear these stories as children and they are still as exciting today.

In addition to these stories, Daniel's book contains descriptions of visions which God allowed Daniel to experience during his time in captivity along with explanations of what the visions meant. The visions often depict rulers or countries in the form of animals whose characteristics communicate the character of the ruler or the nature of the country to us. In addition, Daniel includes prophecies about rulers, wars, conflicts and other events which were revealed to him in dreams or visions. Some of the events Daniel prophesied about actually came to pass in his own lifetime, some were fulfilled in the next few hundred years, and some we are still waiting to see fulfilled.

You might be wondering about how Daniel's prophetic book applies to us, especially today, when what one thinks often counts for more than hard evidence. A glance at the subtitle of the book will give you the answer to your question: 'The Inspiration of Daniel in an Age of Relativism'. This is a book for anyone who wants to understand how to deal with secularism, humanism, pluralism, relativism and other *en vogue* philosophies when we encounter them in our personal lives and in the public square.

Enjoy the journey.

* * *

I am deeply grateful to my friend Rae Mellichamp for writing this study guide to my book *Against the Flow: The Inspiration of Daniel in an Age of Relativism*.

On the basis of his experience running study groups on Daniel, he has also done sterling work in producing an excellent guide to accompany my later book *Friend of God: The Inspiration of Abraham in an Age of Doubt.*

John C. Lennox

How to Use This Guide

This study guide has two essential aims:

1 Each chapter opens with a section that summarises key points from the relevant chapter in John Lennox's book *Against the Flow*. It is assumed that the reader has already read the whole chapter in that book, and the purpose of the summary is to help refresh and reinforce the memory as well as provide pointers for personal reflection or group discussion along the way. This summary section is therefore focused on the content of the relevant chapter in the main book.
2 There then follows a series of application questions designed to get the reader thinking about the ways in which Daniel serves as a model for faithful living today. What have we learned about Daniel and his friends that we can absorb and apply in our own lives as we seek to be faithful followers of Jesus in a world of widespread relativism and scepticism?

The authors hope that readers will find both the summaries and the application questions helpful as they work through the book, while recognising that some may prefer to go straight to the application questions after having read the relevant chapter in *Against the Flow*.

Whichever way you choose to use this guide, may God bless you in your studies!

1

A Matter of History

Daniel 1

In order for us to understand the wonderful book of Daniel, we need some historical background, which we gain from multiple books of the Bible, as well as from ancient history.

Background

The small state of Judah was located at a geographical nexus in the ancient Middle East, where great powers frequently clashed. Listed below are some of the key locations and players of the time.

The countries involved and their respective capitals were:

- Judah: Jerusalem
- Assyria: Nineveh
- Egypt: Rameses
- Babylonia: Babylon
- Media: Ecbatana
- Persia: Susa
- Greece: Athens.

The important rulers of the time were:

- Hezekiah, Josiah, Jehoahaz and Jehoiakim in Judah
- Sennacherib in Assyria
- Nebuchadnezzar in Babylon
- Cyrus the Great and Darius the Mede in Media
- Xerxes in Persia.

The key characters in the text are:

- Nebuchadnezzar
- Daniel
- Daniel's friends.

Daniel and his friends were taken from their families, society and culture. They had to cope with the stress of a new language and customs, a new political system and new laws, as well as a new education system and new beliefs. How did they come to terms with it?

God and history

The siege of Jerusalem by Nebuchadnezzar and the subsequent deportation of Daniel and his friends is described in Daniel 1:1–6. The events are also recorded in ancient Babylonian Chronicles.

Some questions

- Daniel begins with Nebuchadnezzar's siege of Jerusalem in 605 BC and the destruction of Jerusalem in 586 BC. Why would God allow his capital city to be captured and razed? The Jews were God's chosen people and Judah was the nation of Moses the Lawgiver, David and Solomon.
- What would become of God's promise of the Messiah from David's line if the Jews were forsaken?
- If God is real, how could a pagan emperor like Nebuchadnezzar violate God's Temple? Where was God? Or, why did God not intervene?
- Why does history so often take a turn that shakes confidence in the existence of God?

Some things that secular historians might say

- The conquest of Judah was simply one more example of the law of the jungle and its power.
- The idea of the descendants of David being special is no more than tribal myth.
- The Temple in Jerusalem was only a building; a very special building, but nothing more.
- The very idea that God, if there were a God, would be interested in these events is absurd.

Is God involved?

- Daniel's first pronouncement in his book is that God is involved in history (Daniel 1:2).
- Daniel is interested in why these things happened – not just that they happened.
- 'From Augustine till the eighteenth century, history in Europe was written in the belief that divine providence was the key to understanding events.'[1]
- God's providence 'is a living and active agency both in ourselves and in its movement over the length and breadth of history.'[2]
- All history is interpreted. Is there evidence to say that Daniel's interpretation of this part of history is true?

Belief and evidence

- 'Next time somebody tells you that something is true, why not say to them, "What kind of evidence is there for that?" And if they can't give you a good answer, I hope you will think very carefully before you believe a word they say.'[3]
- Dawkins' view is: Science = facts; Faith = no facts. Professor Lennox asks in response, 'What is the evidence that religious faith is not based on evidence?'
- Here is the apostle John's reason for writing his Gospel: 'But these [things] are written so that you may continue to believe that Jesus is the Christ . . .' (John 20:31).
- Paul, in Romans 1:20, declares that nature is the evidence: 'For ever since the world was created, people have seen the earth and sky. Through everything God made, they can clearly see . . .' (NLT).

History and morality

What evidence did Daniel have as the basis for his understanding of history?

- Humans are moral beings made in the image of God.
- The universe is a moral universe.
- The moral character of God demands that he not be neutral.
- The prophets had repeatedly warned the Jews of immorality.
- In our world today, inconsistent moral behaviour of so-called believers is damaging to the Christian faith.
- The Assyrian invasion and deportation is evidence of not heeding God's warnings.

- Jeremiah warned of precisely what would happen in Jeremiah 22:3–9.
- In the end, Judah came to understand that God is interested in the personal history of individuals.

Why did Daniel and his friends have to suffer for other people's actions? There are no easy answers to this question.

- The heart of monotheism is that God, who is outside of history, gives meaning to history.
- Grappling with the moral difficulties of his time is one of the main focuses of Daniel's book.
- Paul's address to the Areopagus underscores the inadequacy of explaining history without God (Acts 17:26–27).
- We gain insight into the relationship between God's involvement in history and human responsibility *through* stories.

Explanatory power

- Daniel does not give a detailed philosophical explanation resolving the tension between God's sovereignty and human responsibility.
- In times of stress it is profoundly reassuring to know that God is not remote from the ups and downs of our lives, even if we can't fully understand why something is happening.
- This should encourage us when our faith in God is being put through severe testing in the face of adverse circumstances.
- 'I have said all these things to keep you from falling away. They will put you out of the synagogues' (John 16:1–2).

What does it mean that God has plans not to harm us?

- What is harm from God's perspective? In Matthew 10:28–31 Jesus makes it clear that the kind of harm that kills the body is not necessarily what God counts as harm.
- What about suffering?
- Death is not the end but a doorway.
- Daniel ends by confidently asserting his hope in the resurrection (Daniel 12:13).
- Daniel lived in the world; he did not live for it.
- One would be a fool to live for a world that did not exist.
- But if another world does exist, one would be a fool not to live for it.

Application questions

1 Why is history so important in understanding the Bible and its characters?

2 For many centuries, people thought that God was involved in world history. What happened in the eighteenth century that changed the way people understand God's role in events? What does this mean to you in terms of your ultimate identity and purpose?

3 Some scholars go to great lengths to keep God out of the picture. Here is just one example mentioned above: 'The very idea that God, if there were a God, would be interested in these events is absurd.' How could this argument be countered?

4 Think about the statement 'The universe is a moral universe'. What arguments can be used to support this statement?

2
City of Idols
Daniel 1

This chapter gives us an overview of the city and the culture into which Daniel and his friends were taken in order to be educated in the ways of the Babylonians.

A spectacular city

Babylon was the largest city in the world at the time. It had been destroyed by Sennacherib of Assyria a century earlier and was rebuilt by the ensuing Babylonian emperors, particularly Nebuchadnezzar (605–561 BC). Nebuchadnezzar's name is inscribed on 90% of the bricks unearthed from the city. Herodotus believed it to be the most beautiful city in the world when he visited it 200 years later.

Some specifics

The city was rectangular in shape, with the Euphrates river flowing north to south through it. Herodotus said its walls were 80 feet thick, 320 feet high and 56 miles long, although archaeologists now dispute these figures. The major gates of the city were named after Babylonian gods, of which there were many.

The Ishtar gate

The magnificent gate was built with a view to impressing all who entered the city with its power, wealth, architecture and permanence. There is a reconstruction of the gate in the Pergamon Museum, Berlin. You can read a translation of Nebuchadnezzar's inscription on the gate on page 29 of *Against the Flow*. The inscription is positioned at the north end of the great Processional Way, which traversed the length of the city.

The temple of Akitu

The temple of Akitu lies just outside the Ishtar gate. The idol of the god Nabu, the god of wisdom, would be brought to the temple every year for important springtime ceremonies.

The ziggurat

The ziggurat would have dominated the skyline: a spectacular tower, reminiscent of the Tower of Babel. It was seven storeys tall and stood 100 metres above street level. The rooms on the highest level were dedicated to Babylonian deities and their wives:

- Marduk, the chief god
- Nabu, the god of wisdom
- Ea, the water god
- Nusku, the god of light
- Anu, the god of heaven.

The roof of the ziggurat probably served as an observatory. The Babylonians were fascinated by astrology.

Buildings on the great Processional Way

- Nebuchadnezzar's palace contained an imposing throne room designed to inspire awe. The palace roof gardens were the famous Hanging Gardens of Babylon, one of the seven wonders of the ancient world.
- Esagila was a huge temple complex dedicated to the supreme god, Marduk.

First impressions

Daniel and his friends must have been struck by the elegance of the architecture and the apparent advanced state of learning in the city. They must also have been struck by the idolatry that permeated society, which would have been visible almost everywhere.

Application questions

1 We are told in Ezra 7:9 that the journey from Babylon to Jerusalem (or from Jerusalem to Babylon) took four months on foot. Imagine these four young men, who have been captured, taken from their homes, families and friends, and had their lives redirected. What do you think they may have thought of and discussed during their journey?

2 Imagine the young men walking into Babylon at the end of the journey. Jerusalem was a beautiful city, but the Babylonians would soon utterly

destroy it. Babylon was described as the most beautiful city in the world. The Euphrates river flowed through it and the city represented a major world power. What impact do you think this may have had on the young men's faith?

3 Babylon's architecture was designed to display power. The walls and gates of the city conveyed the impression of impregnability. The location was strategic – it was on the main river in the region and centrally located. The buildings were situated in order to reinforce the impression of invincibility. How do you think these young men would have reacted upon first walking around the city?

4 The young men were there for a purpose. They were to be trained in the 'literature and language' of the Chaldeans. These young men had been trained in the wisdom of the Jews: God's word, the holy Scriptures. Now they would be trained in the pagan culture of the Babylonians. Do you think they understood the challenge before them? How might this compare with the situation of Christian young people in our schools, colleges and universities today?

5 The overall layout of the city of Babylon and its architecture were intended to draw attention to the Babylonian gods. Temples to these gods were strategically placed throughout the city. What do you think Daniel and his friends would have made of this?

6 The ziggurat reminds us of the Tower of Babel in Genesis 11, which was built by the Sumerians (forerunners of the Babylonians) as a tower to 'reach into heaven'. The tower was long gone by the time of Daniel but the arrogance of the people still seems to have been in play. How can we see this?

7 Daniel, Hananiah, Mishael and Azariah found themselves in the midst of
this pagan city ready, as it were, to begin college. Their experiences and
God's incredible works in their lives and in world history are the subject
of this remarkable book. What inspires or encourages you most about
them?

3
A Question of Values
Daniel 1

And the Lord gave Jehoiakim king of Judah into his [Nebuchadnezzar's] hand, with some of the vessels of the house of God. And he brought them to the land of Shinar [Babylon], to the house of his god, and placed the vessels in the treasury of his god.

(Daniel 1:2)

Nebuchadnezzar takes vessels from the Temple

The fact that Nebuchadnezzar took vessels from the Temple in Jerusalem may seem a detail of little significance. But was it? Why is this mentioned in the biblical account? Nebuchadnezzar had a treasure house, possibly in the Esagila temple complex (the house of his god), where 'booty' from across his empire was stored and potentially displayed. Many of these artefacts are now on display in museums around the world. In Ezra 1:11, we learn that 5,400 gold and silver vessels were taken from the Temple.

A question of values

The vessels Nebuchadnezzar took from the Temple were used for worship and considered holy – set apart for the glory of God.

- Gold was the most precious metal known at the time.
- God is the supreme value for men and women.

In our worship

- Do we appreciate what sacredness is?
- Do we set apart God's name as holy (hallow his name)?
- Is God of supreme value to us?

What was the significance of the vessels for the four exiles?

- They represented all that was central to their worship.
- They were a tangible link to the Temple.
- They were a reminder of Israel's fall.
- They reminded them of how much Israel had lost. (A sense of the glory and holiness of God.)

What are the lessons for us today?

- Many people do not honour God.
- Holiness has become a negative concept to many and is thought to be drab and lifeless.
- The awe of the holiness of God, which the Temple was built to convey, is easily lost.
- Symbols that once pointed to spiritual realities can tend to become ends in themselves.
- Admiration of church architecture, art and ritual is not the same as the worship of a glorious God.

For the exiles the golden vessels would have been:

- points of light in a dark world
- reminders of the value system they embraced.

Relativising the absolute

Nebuchadnezzar placed the Temple vessels in the treasure house of the temple of *his* god. To him they were simply artefacts from one of his conquests. To him, they and other artefacts illustrated the superiority of both himself and his gods. Daniel's prominent mention of the vessels at the beginning of his book may be because it illustrates taking something of absolute value and reducing it to something of relative value. The vessels were symbols that pointed to the one true God, but they were placed with cultic symbols of other gods.

Relativisation of the absolute is endemic today in our 'pick and mix' society. Take your pick: Jesus, Buddha, celebrity culture, 'Mother Earth' or crystals – all are held on the same footing for the relativist.

- Absolutes are thought dangerous by many.
- Religious faith is seen as responsible for much strife.
- Atheism is regarded as the only defensible alternative.

We should remember:

- Defence of a country or nation is different from defence of Jesus and his message.
- When Jesus was put on trial he was charged with fomenting terrorism, but Pilate publicly declared him 'not guilty'.
- Use of force to impose Christ's message defies his explicit commands and makes many deaf to his message.

Relativising truth

Any relativising tendency in culture affects values and ultimately affects truth. At the heart of postmodernism lies a patent self-contradiction. We are asked to accept as absolute truth that there are no absolute truths. However, it is clear that everyone has to live their life around certain absolute truths (such as their bank balance).

Application questions

1 Most of us have probably read the book of Daniel several times. Have you noticed the taking of the Temple vessels before? What is its significance?

2 The sheer number of vessels in the loot which Nebuchadnezzar took from the Temple in Jerusalem is impressive – 5,400. Such a collection would demand to be put on display in a prominent place in Babylon, presumably in the Esagila temple. In doing this, what is implicitly being said about the two cultures and their gods?

3 Daniel and his friends knew that the vessels were holy and set apart for the glory of God. They also knew that God should be the supreme value for all people. How did they understand this, and yet *we* sometimes completely miss it?

4 Do you agree that in our time we have lost a sense of the glory and holiness of God? Can you give some examples?

5 There are many people in the world today who admire church architecture, religious art and ritual. But this is far from worshipping the glorious God for whom these things were created. What can we do to reverse the tide of this lost sensitivity towards the one true God?

6 How did Nebuchadnezzar relativise the absolute?

7 Postmodernism is based on the absolute truth that there are no absolutes. How can this attitude about truth impact culture?

4

A Question of Identity

Daniel 1

Nebuchadnezzar was a ruthless, absolute monarch, who chose the most able of his captives and trained them for service as representatives of the government in Babylon.

The attributes he looked for in his captive trainees were:

- youth (so they were not set in their ways)
- physical fitness and beauty
- strong intellectual, administrative aptitudes
- the capacity to learn his language and culture.

Once trained, some would return to their home countries as ambassadors of the new culture. Daniel and his friends were so outstanding that they were ordered to remain in Babylon.

What's in a name?

Changing the captives' names from Hebrew to Babylonian names was a form of social engineering. Hebrew names would not only make the captives stand out, but they were also loaded with meaning that bore witness to God.

- Daniel means God is my judge.
- Hananiah means the Lord shows grace.
- Mishael means who is like God?
- Azariah means the Lord helps.

Ashpenaz, Nebuchadnezzar's official, gave the four captives these new Babylonian names:

- Daniel – Beltshazzar, which means may Bel (Marduk) protect his life.
- Hananiah – Shadrach, which means command of Aku (the moon god).
- Azariah – Abednego, which means servant of Nabu (son of Marduk).
- Mishael – Meshach, which means who is like Aku? (the moon god).

The significance of this for the four friends? Babylon could change their names, but Babylon could not change their identities or their hearts.

Babylon and the search for meaning

What was at the heart of Babylon as a city?

The people of Babylon were striving to find meaning through science and through architecture (Genesis 11:1-4). But they were looking in the wrong place. Meaning is found in God's call – this alone endows life with meaning.

We see earlier in the Old Testament that where the people of Babel trusted in their own abilities, Abraham accepted God for his significance.

'Who am I?' is one of life's deepest questions.

- Psychologist Nola Passmore says: 'The heart cry of the human race is for meaning and purpose.'
- Psychotherapist and Holocaust survivor Viktor Frankl says in his book *Man's Search for Meaning*: 'Humans derive their ultimate significance from being made in the image of God.'[4]

There is an interesting parallel between Abraham and Daniel.

- Abraham was called out of Mesopotamia by God.
- Daniel was forcibly taken to Mesopotamia, where he witnessed to the land that Abraham had left.

The confusion of language

The origins of Babylon are recorded in Genesis 11:5-9 and the story of the Tower of Babel, in which God scatters the people and 'confuses' their language so that they can't understand one another. In effect, Nebuchadnezzar attempts to reverse this, and even the young men's Hebrew names are taken from them.

Relativism today

- Professor Lennox suggests that we are 'deconstructing the nature of human beings and the society we live in' (*Against the Flow, p. 55*).
- Cardinal Ratzinger, before he became Pope Benedict XVI, warned that 'We are building [a world] that does not recognise anything as definitive and whose ultimate goal consists solely of one's own ego and desires.'[5]

Application questions

1 Nebuchadnezzar had a motive in bringing captive young men to Babylon to educate them in the language and literature of the Babylonians – to make them insiders, rather than outsiders. Can you explain this?

2 The hypothetical conversation that Professor Lennox includes between the four Hebrew men and the four Babylonian men in which the Hebrews talk about the meaning of their names is a powerful way of underscoring the importance of names and the implications of the names for the faith of these young men. How does this relate to cultural assimilation today?

3 Biblical names are often packed with meaning. Is this still the same for our names today?

4 Being made in the image of God had powerful implications for thoughtful people then and now as well. It is this attribute which makes us responsible (accountable) to God for our lives – in both our actions and words. And it is this accountability which gives our lives purpose and meaning. How can you ensure that you recognise this in your life?

5 Judgement and accountability are absolutely necessary in life. If there is no judgement, then there is no accountability, and accountability confers dignity and value. How do you think we are doing as a society today on judgement and accountability?

6 The example of Babel and God 'confusing' language is a powerful way
   of bringing up the issue of relativism. When we are irresponsible with
   language – words and definitions – anything goes. Can you think of ways
   in which this is happening today?

5

The Resolution and the Protest

Daniel 1

Daniel and his friends may not have had an opportunity to oppose being given new names. But they soon had an opportunity to witness for God.

A student of holiness

Food

The students were given the very best food – the same food that was served to the emperor himself. The students from the besieged city of Jerusalem had probably never seen anything like it. They would have been used to wartime rations.

But in Daniel 1:8, we learn that 'Daniel resolved that he would not defile himself with the king's food'. This was an inward resolution of heart and mind that preceded his outward action.

Holiness

Daniel's choice arose from his convictions about holiness. Because of his dedication and commitment to God, Daniel wanted his personality and character to be moulded by God's holiness. Peter captured the essence of Daniel's challenge centuries later in 1 Peter 3:14–16. Both Peter and Daniel find themselves in situations where they are asked to stand out from the crowd and make public expressions of their faith.

Persuading others that God is real requires:

- personal loyalty to God and his Son
- living lives consistent with our confession.

Daniel would also have been aware that God had frequently warned Israel, through a succession of prophets, of the dangers and consequences of being defiled by the practices of neighbouring pagan cultures.

In the New Testament God warns us of similar dangers that remain ever present in our society.

The food laws

God had given Israel food laws that prohibited certain unclean foods. This would have made mixing with people from other cultures, who did not follow such laws, difficult.

Why did God give Israel food laws?

In Paul's letter to the Galatians, he explains that just as in ancient custom children had a guardian to protect them until maturity, Israel had the law as a guardian until the coming of Christ.

- God treated the infant nation of Israel as a child, guarding it with rules and regulations.

The problem with this framework of rules is that those who were brought up under it could fall into the error of confusing obedience to the rules concerning outward ceremonial cleanness with real inner moral cleanness.

When Jesus came, he cancelled this system of rules. And the Holy Spirit came

- to give believers the inner power to resist corruption,
- so they could mingle with other cultures and resist the pressures of evil thoughts and behaviour.

The laws also prohibited eating blood and blood products in order to remind Israel of the sanctity of life.

A choice: God or idols?

A third reason for Daniel's stand may have been that

- the food had been sacrificed to idols,
- or it had been ceremonially involved with pagan rituals.

On this topic, see the Georges Roux quote in *Against the Flow* on page 62.

Babylon had more than 1,000 pagan temples, and there are likely to have been constant offerings to other gods (for an example see Daniel 5). Daniel refused to be involved with such rituals, thus protesting against the Babylonian worldview, which formed the background paradigm of their education system.

Application questions

1 Can you imagine four university students today not eating delicious food in order to make a statement about personal purity? Can you think of any modern-day examples of someone taking a similar stand for their faith?

2 Defilement is breaking an inward resolution of heart and mind arising from convictions about holiness. Daniel wanted his personality and character to be moulded by God's holiness. He felt that the food offered them would be a distraction. How could this be?

3 In 1 Peter 3:14–16 we are advised to be ready to defend our faith. Do you see how Daniel and his friends were gearing up to do this very thing over the food issue? Did they have a chance to make their arguments? Were they successful?

4 Give some examples of the existence of the pagan culture around us today. Have you done any homework on these? Are you ready to defend Christian positions on these issues vis-à-vis pagan practices? What do you need to do here?

5 What do you think about the food laws outlined above? God gave them to the Jewish people to protect them from the influences of pagan cultures and to make it difficult for his people to mingle with pagan corruption. How might keeping the food laws be confused with cultivating real inner moral cleanliness? Can you think of any similar applications for you today?

6 The food laws were cancelled by Jesus when he was here among us. He taught that the Holy Spirit was given to us to empower us to resist inner corruption. Can you share any examples of the working of God's Spirit in you in this connection?

7 The bottom line is that with Christ's coming and the abolition of the law we are able to associate with unbelievers to give us an opportunity to share our faith with them. Can you give an illustration of how this has worked in your own experience?

6
The World-view of Babylon
Daniel 1

God, the gods and the universe

So, what was the Babylonian world-view and how did it contrast with that of Daniel?

- Daniel believed that there was one true God, the Creator of heaven and earth. The Babylonians believed that there were many gods. The Babylonian creation epic, the *Enuma Elish*, describes the origins of the universe (cosmogony) and the origins of the gods (theogony).
- The Babylonian theogony describes how the gods emerged out of freshwater and saltwater. They were part of the material stuff of the universe, although in Babylonian mythology the very beginning may go back to Nammu, the mother who gave birth to the universe.
- Greek theogony displays similar ideas about a race of venerable gods arising.
- The key difference between Hebrew and Greek/Babylonian belief is that the Greek/Babylonian gods are stationed *inside* the world and are descended from heaven and earth. The God of the Hebrews is *outside* of the world and gives meaning to it.
- It is not matter that is eternal and self-existent, but God (who is Spirit).

Materialistic reductionism is alive and well

So, how close is the Babylonian model to current thinking? The idea that mass-energy is primitive and that everything else derives from it is the essence of materialistic reductionism that tries to dominate Western society. It is ironic that those who won't accept God ascribe the creative powers to blind, unguided material processes. Even those scientists, such as Paul Davies, who recognise the 'fine tuning' of the universe are likely to ascribe this to natural rather than supernatural causes.

Understanding the surrounding world-view

Daniel and his friends did not protest against the education they were given. In fact, he and his friends were star pupils.

- Daniel did not protest as an observer, but as a participant.
- Daniel's understanding of God was biblical (see Jeremiah 29:1–14) and did not lead to a ghetto mentality, but instead led him to a full and prominent life.
- Daniel and his friends did not forget Jerusalem and all it stood for.
- They sought the wellbeing of the city as salt and light.

The language of protest

If we are convinced of the biblical world-view, shouldn't we protest against the secularism that threatens to engulf us in the West? The battle takes place in the thought-world, in the realm of ideas and world-views, not in the realm of military weaponry (2 Corinthians 13:3–5).

We are called to give a reasoned argument for our faith,

- to be apologists
- to be defenders.

A call to commitment

Because of the nature of the battle, loyalty to Jesus Christ is a prerequisite: moral, intellectual and spiritual loyalty. Paul outlined the intellectual and spiritual commitment to Christ required in 2 Corinthians 11:2–4 in terms of 'betrothal' – a binding oath. In Corinth believers had pledged their lives to Christ, but as time went on, Paul heard rumours that their loyalty to Christ was being undermined or watered down by other ideas. The same can be true of us today. The idea of the uniqueness of Christ and many defining doctrines of Christianity are under attack as they have never been before. Many have abandoned belief in:

- the pre-existence of Christ
- Christ's supernatural conception, miracles, and so on.

We need to listen to God. That is Daniel's challenge to us!

Application questions

1 The underlying point of dissension in the book of Daniel is a clash of world-views. Daniel and his friends believed there is only one God – the Creator of heaven and earth. The Babylonians believed in many gods and had stories of how the creation came to be. How is this division still in play today?

2 The significant difference between these two positions is the location of God or the gods with respect to the creation. If the gods are a part of the creation, they can have no impact on the creation itself, they are simply part of it. If God is outside of the creation, he can use it for his purposes. How would you explain this?

3 'Materialist reductionism' is a big term, but we do not need to be intimidated by it. It simply means that matter is everything. Everything else derives from the interactions of matter according to universal laws. Was this belief as relevant in Daniel's time as it is in ours? Can you explain?

4 The *idea* that the universe looks as though it was fine tuned to support life as we know it is known as the anthropic principle. If any of the universal constants changed ever so slightly, life as we know it would be impossible. Many think this is a powerful argument for God's involvement in creation. What do you think?

5 Understanding the surrounding world-view was the task to which Daniel and his friends committed themselves and it must be the task of every thinking believer. How much time and energy have you expended on understanding the prevalent world-view in the world today? How could you improve your understanding?

6 In the prophecy of Jeremiah, God commanded the Jewish exiles to Babylon to 'seek the welfare of the city where I have sent you into exile, and pray to the Lord on its behalf, for in its welfare you will find your welfare' (Jeremiah 29:7). Did Daniel and his friends obey the command?

7 'Apologetics' and 'apologists' are words that cause some believers to shrink back today. Why do you think that is so? In 2 Corinthians 10:3–5 we are charged to 'destroy arguments and every lofty opinion raised against the knowledge of God'. How? By giving an *apologia* (defence) for our faith, just as the four Hebrew men did. How are you doing this?

7

The Manner of the Protest

Daniel 1

Have no fear of them, nor be troubled, but in your hearts honour Christ the Lord as holy [or 'sanctify Christ in your hearts'], always being prepared to make a defence to anyone who asks you for a reason for the hope that is in you; yet do it with gentleness and respect, having a good conscience, so that, when you are slandered, those who revile your good behaviour in Christ will be put to shame.

(1 Peter 3:14–16)

The need for sensitivity

The way in which Daniel made his protest is a model for us. We are to defend the message with 'gentleness and respect'.

Daniel follows this approach:

- He speaks to Ashpenaz privately.
- He asks for permission not to take the food and defile himself.

He does not:

- make a public display in the dining room and demand alternative food as a right.

Ashpenaz's response is equally honest:

- He is fearful he will be in trouble with the king and admits this to Daniel.

However, God gives Daniel favour and compassion in the eyes of Ashpenaz. Think about your tone. Might it be seen as:

- an aggressive tone reeking of superiority
- off-putting to others
- entirely unlike that of Jesus, who was gentle and humble (Matthew 11:29), and courteous and respectful?

We want people to know that God loved the world in such a way that he gave his Son to die for it. This is not done by showing disrespect to others.
This doesn't mean that we have to

- condone all they do
- expose their sin so that they might repent.

Jesus was sensitive in a magnificent way. He left us footsteps to follow and we need to be faithful in this.

A quiet confidence

Ashpenaz trusts Daniel enough to tell him that he fears the wrath of the king if Daniel and his friends begin to look unhealthy (Daniel 1:10).
So Daniel tries his Plan B.

- He asks Ashpenaz's deputy if they can do a controlled experiment and not eat the king's food for a period of ten days, to see if they really would look unhealthy as a result.

Some lessons for us:

- Daniel took his time and trusted God.
- He was sensitive to other people's concerns.
- Daniel gave the deputy space and time to test things out.
- Daniel and his friends were prepared to pay whatever the cost in order to maintain God as their supreme value.
- Just as God equipped the four young men for their roles, he will equip us for ours. Each of us has a different function, and each function is necessary and valuable.
- We must trust God for our significance.
- Contentment comes from understanding that it pleased God to make us as we are.

Application questions

1 One does not have to strain to understand that this is an extremely sensitive situation. There was a famous slogan used in propaganda material during the Second World War which stated, 'Careless talk costs lives.' This captures the delicacy of the situation at hand. If Daniel and his friends are not sensitive and discreet the whole undertaking might come unstuck. Can you think of ways in which carelessly stating our case could cost lives for Christ?

2 Daniel goes to Ashpenaz privately with a counter proposal. Would he allow Daniel and his friends to follow a different diet (Daniel 1:8)? Daniel had apparently had enough interaction with Ashpenaz to earn his respect and compassion. Why do you think this might be?

3 Why do you think Ashpenaz is so afraid? In what circumstances might you be afraid of doing the right thing?

4 We always need to remind ourselves of our objective. We want people to understand that God loves the world and he gave his one and only Son to die for it. This is not a competition. It is far, far more significant. Why do you think Jesus' reputation for gentleness (see Matthew 11:29, for example) is appropriate here?

5 Daniel has a Plan B (Daniel 1:11–13). He talks the situation over with the official who is directly in charge of the Hebrew young men. Daniel offers him a controlled scientific experiment: 'Test your servants for ten days; let us be given vegetables to eat and water to drink. Then let our appearance and the appearance of the youths who eat the king's food be

observed by you.' How does Daniel's approach demonstrate wisdom and how can we apply that to our own problems?

6 Ultimately, our significance is in God's hands. Not many of us will be Daniels. Possibly the best advice for us in this regard will be to hear Jesus say to us, 'Well done, good and faithful servant.' That will be enough. How are you exploring your place in God's plan?

8
The Logical Structure of Daniel

A tale of two languages

Compared to other prophetic works in the Bible, Daniel is a relatively short book. Interestingly it was written in two languages – Aramaic and Hebrew.

- Daniel 1:1 – 2:3 and 8:1 – 12:13 is in Hebrew.
- Daniel 2:3 – 7:28 is in Aramaic.

The text itself does not tell us why this was done and there are various explanations given by scholars. Here is what we do know for sure:

- Aramaic was the *lingua franca* of the day. This part of Daniel includes a statement written in the first person by Nebuchadnezzar, explaining how he came to know the one true God. This would have been useful to the exiles as they witnessed to the Babylonians.
- Hebrew, of course, was the language of the Jews, so it would have been natural for the remainder of the story to have been written in Hebrew.

Topics of Daniel

Here is a topical list of the contents of the book of Daniel.

1 Daniel refuses the king's food.
2 Nebuchadnezzar's dream – the image.
3 Nebuchadnezzar's golden image; the fiery furnace.
4 Discipline and restoration of Nebuchadnezzar.
5 Judgement of Belshazzar; Babylon's end.
6 Daniel refuses to pray to Darius; the lions' den.
7 Daniel's vision of four beasts.
8 Daniel's vision of two animals.
9 Jeremiah's prophecy about Jerusalem; Daniel's prayer.
10 The writing of truth; the end of time.

Detecting a pattern

Looking through the list of topics above, we can see that the book divides into two major sections, with similar events under each section. Here is what that looks like:

1 Daniel: the first part
    (a) A court scene. Daniel's refusal to eat.
    (b) Two images of enormous proportions:
        (i) The image of Nebuchadnezzar's dream.
        (ii) The image of Nebuchadnezzar's statue.
    (c) Two kings are disciplined.
        (i) Nebuchadnezzar is humbled because of pride.
        (ii) Belshazzar is judged because of arrogance.
        (iii) The fall of Babylon is a backdrop to part one, including Nebuchadnezzar's prominent role and the golden vessels and moral values.

2 Daniel: the second part
    (a) A court scene. Daniel's refusal to pray.
    (b) Two visions of strange animals:
        (i) Four beasts (chapter 7).
        (ii) Two beasts (chapter 8).
    (c) Two writings are explained.
        (i) The prophecy of Jeremiah.
        (ii) The writings of truth.

This creates a side-by-side arrangement.

Part A	Part B
Court scene	*Court scene*
Chapter 1	**Chapter 6**
Babylonian court	Medo-Persian court
Daniel refuses to eat the king's food.	Daniel refuses to obey the king's command and refrain from praying to God.
He and his friends are vindicated.	He is vindicated.
Two images	*Two visions of beasts*
Chapter 2	**Chapter 7**
Nebuchadnezzar's dream	Four beasts
Chapter 3	**Chapter 8**
Nebuchadnezzar's image	Two beasts
Two kings disciplined	*Two writings explained*
Chapter 4	**Chapter 9**
Discipline and restoration of Nebuchadnezzar	The prophecy in Jeremiah about the destruction and restoration of Jerusalem
Chapter 5	**Chapters 10–12**
The 'writing on the wall' and death of Belshazzar	The 'Writing of Truth' and the eventual destruction of 'the king'
The end of Babylonian supremacy	The end of world history

Application questions

1 In part one we have the court scene, the two images (Nebuchadnezzar's dream and his idol of himself) and then the two kings disciplined (Nebuchadnezzar and Belshazzar). Nebuchadnezzar had an opportunity to repent whereas Belshazzar did not. Do you think you might see Nebuchadnezzar in the future? We are told that the backdrop of part one is the destruction of Babylon. Do you think this was prophetic?

2 The 2 x 2 groupings are helpful. In part one we have two images and two kings, while in part two we have two visions and two writings explained. Did this help your understanding? How?

3 The 2 x 2 grouping is also seen in Jeremiah's prophecy (the first of the writings) and the second 'writing of truth'; that is, the material contained in chapters 10–12 of Daniel which deal with the end times of the earth. What do you deduce from this layout?

4 So, the bottom line for us from chapter 8 of *Against the Flow* is that the side-by-side outline organises the material in such a way that we will be able to understand it as we cover it – not sequentially but topically in a parallel scheme that is constructed logically. What are your impressions of this way of looking at the book?

9
Dreams and Revelations
Daniel 2

Nebuchadnezzar is mentioned in the first five chapters of the book of Daniel. Chapter 4 consists of Nebuchadnezzar's own testimony. Chapter 5 shows Belshazzar being disciplined by God because he had deliberately turned away from God, despite knowing what had happened to Nebuchadnezzar.

The flow of chapters 1–4 relates a dawning on Nebuchadnezzar:

- of the reality of God
- on his mind and heart
- leading to his 'conversion'.

Chapter 2 addresses the question as to whether there is such a thing as supernatural revelation.

- Daniel's answer to this question is a major challenge to contemporary secularism, which insists that the universe is a closed system of cause and effect.

Revelation and dating the book of Daniel

The dating of the book of Daniel has been a matter of major controversy. The controversy lies in the fact that Daniel made predictions about what would happen in the centuries to come. And the predictions he made turned out to be correct.

Even today authors and filmmakers write about the future and predict what may happen. Some famous examples include George Orwell's *1984* and Aldous Huxley's *Brave New World*. Some of the predictions made in these works have come true. However, the problem for some people is that Daniel got too much of it right!

Daniel outlines the breakdown of the Babylonian empire and the subsequent history of the region. Although he does not name characters, he does give details of some of the complex relationships of the Seleucids and Ptolemies, and of later periods of Hellenistic history. He got it absolutely right!

Some scholars argue that there is no way Daniel could have made these accurate predictions, unless he had lived after the fact and was writing history rather than revelation. Thus, in their opinion, the book must have been written in the second century BC and not in the 605–535 BC timeframe.

Revealing and interpreting Nebuchadnezzar's dream

It started with Nebuchadnezzar's dream. Instead of just asking his advisors to interpret his dream, he told the advisors that they must not only interpret his dream, but also tell him what the dream itself was. If they are unable to do this, he would put them to death.

Understandably, the response of the king's advisors was, 'This is impossible!'

- They did not believe in revelation from the gods.
- They did not believe that the gods communicated with humans.
- Their universe was a closed system in which cause and effect was everything.
- Their epistemology was the same as that of the Enlightenment.

However, Daniel's response was different. When Arioch, the king's captain, comes to tell Daniel and his friends that they are to be executed, he discovers the cause of the king's decree, and then asks for a little time, so that he can do what the king has requested.

Daniel persuades Arioch to delay his action.

- He requests an audience with Nebuchadnezzar.
- He requests prayer from his friends.

Reason and revelation

What is the relationship between reason and revelation? Atheist thinkers often pit these ideas against one another as if revelation is anti-reason.

- The king's advisors would have applied their reason to the king's dream, had he revealed it, but he chose not to.
- Reason without revelation was unable to provide answers.

However, Daniel believed that God could reveal to him what the king's dream was, as well as its meaning.

- God revealed the dream to Daniel.
- Daniel still had to use his reason to understand what God said and form a response to the king.
- The king had to use his reason to understand that Daniel did know his dream and that his interpretation made sense.

Why should we believe in revelation?

Peter gives us testimony to the other real and eternal dimension in 2 Peter 1:14 when he recalls the transfiguration. Prophecy is from God and assures us of God's eternal kingdom so that we might invest our lives in it.

The supernatural origin of biblical prophecy

The fulfilment of prophecy lies at the heart of Christianity. Many of Christianity's central events were the subject of prophetic predictions.

Contemporary culture in the West is dominated by naturalism. Richard Dawkins' view, as stated in *The God Delusion,* is that either we believe in miracles, or we believe in science, but we cannot believe in both. See quote in *Against the Flow* on page 99. However, there are many scientists who do believe in both!

The dating of Daniel revisited

There are a number of reasons for arguing for an earlier date than the second century BC.

- The testimony of the Dead Sea Scrolls discovered at Qumran.
- Daniel was canonical by 100 BC.
- There is no reason for considering a second-century-BC date.

Daniel's view of revelation

- God reveals deep and hidden things only he knows.
- God is sovereign and intervenes in response to prayer.

Application questions

1 Chapter 2 addresses the question of revelation, such as 'Does God actually reveal future events to individuals (prophets)?' Your answer to this question will shape your understanding of Christianity. How is this so?

2 The logic of many today regarding the date of Daniel's writing is that Daniel's predictions of world events from his time forward must have been made after the fact since they were so accurate. He was writing history, not prophecy. What do you think of this statement?

3 The story of Nebuchadnezzar asking his advisors to interpret his dream – but under a new set of rules – is clever. 'You tell me the dream, then tell me the interpretation' should have been standard operating procedure. Why wasn't it?

4 We have to admire Daniel for believing that God would reveal the king's dream to him. If God hadn't revealed the dream to Daniel, Daniel would have died. Was Daniel foolish, or did he have great faith? Put yourself in Daniel's position. What would you have done?

5 Have you thought about why the revelation was given of God's eternal kingdom? Are you investing your life in the kingdom? In what ways?

6 What do you think of the evidence presented for a date of 605–535 BC for Daniel's writing? Is it a strong case, thanks to the discovery of the Dead Sea Scrolls?

10

A Succession of Empires

Daniel 2

Once God had revealed the information that Nebuchadnezzar required to Daniel, he worked with Arioch to prevent the executions. In a generous move he considered all the condemned, not just his fellow countrymen. Nebuchadnezzar's wise men were Daniel's seniors and indeed, in the future, they would become his enemies. This is an important principle. Daniel disagreed with the world-view of the king's advisors, but he intervened to save their lives. This is a lesson in true tolerance. We may disagree with the views of others, but we should support their right to hold their views. To do otherwise is to prohibit free speech.

In return, Arioch respected Daniel enough to take a risk and get him an audience with the king. Daniel had complete confidence in what God had revealed to him.

God designed prophecy so that when we read it, we know it is from him. Daniel believed God's revelation and interpretation.

Daniel before the king

Arioch announces that he has 'found among the exiles from Judah a man who will make known to the king the interpretation'.

Nebuchadnezzar asks if Daniel is 'able to make known to [him] the dream that [he has] seen and its interpretation' (2:26).

Daniel's answer is carefully worded to draw out the difference between himself and the 'wise men' and to make clear that it is God who has revealed everything to him. 'No wise men, enchanters, magicians, or astrologers can show to the king the mystery that the king has asked, but there is a God in heaven who reveals mysteries' (2:27–28).

Daniel unashamedly witnesses to his faith in front of this mighty ruler. Nebuchadnezzar's city is full of temples to various gods, but none of them is able to 'reveal mysteries' like Daniel's God. Daniel makes it clear that he doesn't make the dream and its interpretation known to the king out of self-interest, 'not because of any wisdom that I have more than all the living' (2:30), but so that the king might know that God is interested in him and wants him to know it. According to the Babylonian world-view there was no god who could reveal the future course of history.

But there is a God who knows. Daniel's God had revealed Nebuchadnezzar's dream of a terrifying statue.

The statue was of a colossal man who had:

- a head of gold
- a chest and arms of silver
- a middle and thighs of bronze
- legs of iron
- feet made of a mixture of iron and clay.

A crashing stone then came and struck the statue at its weakest point, the feet, and completely destroyed it, while the stone itself became a 'great mountain', eventually filling the whole world.

No wonder Nebuchadnezzar didn't want to reveal the contents of his dream to his advisors if he suspected that it meant he as the 'biggest man' in the empire might be toppled. However, there were further puzzles for Nebuchadnezzar.

- What did the metals signify?
- What was wrong with the feet?
- What was the crashing stone?

Which inevitably led to the question of what else Daniel knew.

The interpretation of the dream

Daniel begins on a positive note, telling the king that he himself is the statue's head of gold. Nebuchadnezzar's kingdom was both golden and glorious and given to him by God, as Daniel explains (see also Romans 13:1).

The implications of this are that:

- Nebuchadnezzar's kingdom is neither permanent nor absolute.
- As the whole statue does not represent him, he will have successors.

Perhaps surprisingly, the king does not immediately have Daniel executed for treason for suggesting that Nebuchadnezzar's empire will have an end. Instead, Nebuchadnezzar recognises that Daniel has the wisdom and authority that he himself does not.

So, what were the empires represented by the different parts of the statue? From a historical perspective we know that the Babylonian empire gave way to the Medo-Persian empire, which would last 200 years.

- Daniel himself would experience this transition.
- The law that replaced Babylonian law was that of the Medes and Persians, rather than just the Medes (Daniel 6:8, 12).
- The ram of Daniel 8 is identified to be the kings of Media and Persia.

Following on from the Medo-Persian empire was the Greek empire, which lasted around 130 years.

- The goat of Daniel 8 is identified as Greece.

The transition from the Greek to the Roman empire interestingly corresponds with the move from the Bronze Age to the Iron Age.

The Roman empire lasted a long time in various forms:

- the western Roman empire until AD 476
- the eastern empire (Byzantium) until AD 1453.

Its legacy is still with us.

- Latin was the language of science right up until the eighteenth century.
- Roman law influences current law.
- Latin script is used for most European languages.

The symbolism of the metals for each empire moves from prediction into interpretation. Each metal displays different strengths and weaknesses.

- Babylon as an empire of gold had an aura of splendour.
- The iron empire of Rome, however, was strong and efficient.
- No system of government has absolute value.
- Kingdoms often fail because of arrogance. (See Herbert Butterfield quote in *Against the Flow*, page 113.[6])

The four empires all contributed to society, but Daniel does not give equal prominence to each. The first and fourth are given the most emphasis.

- The God of heaven will set up his kingdom.
- God has made known to the king what will happen.

The stone and the kingdom

The stone of Nebuchadnezzar's dream is quite separate from the statue – it comes from elsewhere. This is the kingdom of God.

- It is not an empire like the others.
- It is not a final stage of world government.
- It is, however, a supernatural kingdom (cut out 'by no human hand', 2:45), which replaces all world empires, and is brought into existence by God.

What would the stone have suggested?

- Stone was not common around Babylon – most of its buildings were made of clay bricks.
- Stone was solid and lasting.

Some scriptural metaphors from the New Testament:

- Simon is renamed 'Cephas', the Aramaic for 'stone'.
- Jesus was 'the stone that the builders rejected' but became the cornerstone (1 Peter 2:4–8).
- The cornerstone (Luke 20:9–18).

Some therefore suggest that the falling of the stone in Daniel 2 refers to the coming of Christ into the world, when he announced his kingdom – a kingdom that gradually grows.

However, Jesus also talks about the 'times of the Gentiles' being fulfilled and being connected with the return of Christ (Luke 21:24–28). So does this instead indicate the time when Christ, the stone, returns to set up his kingdom?

The instability of human governments

It is the instability of the materials making up the statue's feet that causes its downfall. Iron alone would have been strong but iron mixed with clay makes it vulnerable. So what is this pointing to?

- The invasion of the Roman empire?
- The mingling of types of government where iron could symbolise autocratic rule, and clay democratic?

The claim of the book of Daniel is that there are absolute values which stem from God himself. An acid test for leadership is commitment to God's values. In the Western world today we are faced with secularist marginalisation of religion in general, and Christian values in particular, which raises the question: If the majority decides against absolutes, where does that leave the believing minority?

Feet of clay

This term is now often used of individuals of high status, to describe a character fault that could cause downfall. The statue Nebuchadnezzar saw had feet of clay – all systems of government do – caused by the weakness in humanity itself.

The problem with humanity

The problem with humanity is humanity itself – there is a flaw in human nature:

- selfishness and self-centredness
- we still need the boundaries of law for restraint.

Christianity alone attacks the seat of evil.

- Even though human nature is flawed, people insist on placing faith in it.

Rejection of the supernatural lies at the heart of secular humanism.

Secular humanism

Humanism is a view of the world that rejects all religious beliefs. To acknowledge any being as superior would be to compromise humanity's autonomy. To the humanist 'man is the measure of all things'.[7] If we define an idol as anything we trust other than God, then this is clearly idolatry.

Nebuchadnezzar's vision can help guide us by contrasting fatally flawed humanity (the statue) with the stable stone of supernatural origin: humanity transformed by God's supernatural power (see John 3:3).

The Christian view is radical:

- Sin has alienated us from God.
- God, in Christ, has taken the burden from us.
- We can now receive a new supernatural life.

Nebuchadnezzar's response

Nebuchadnezzar must have found himself in a quandary. He thought he understood and controlled the world, but he discovered, through Daniel, that there was another realm which he did not know; one on which he unconsciously depended.

Nebuchadnezzar's reaction

Nebuchadnezzar fell down and worshipped Daniel, saying, 'Truly, your God is God of gods and Lord of kings, and a revealer of mysteries' (2:47). He had discovered that God is real.

Nebuchadnezzar rewarded Daniel by:

- promoting him to high office
- relying on him as his advisor
- promoting his three friends.

The reaction of atheists

Atheists demand evidence for the existence of God and yet some are reluctant to give serious attention to the evidence provided. Those atheistic thinkers who try to discredit Daniel, by claiming that he must have been writing in the second century BC, are perhaps unsettled that he got his facts right.

Application questions

1 We must admire Daniel for believing that God would reveal the details of the dream to him along with its interpretation. Look again at the text. Do you see that Daniel committed himself to revealing the dream to Nebuchadnezzar before God revealed it to him? If he had misjudged God, he would be gone. What do you think?

2 When you think about it, there are logically only two beings who could possibly know one's dreams – the dreamer and, if there is an all-powerful, all-knowing God, then God too. Do you think the king understood this? Once the dream was revealed, would this have had an impact on his beliefs? How so?

3 Nebuchadnezzar was an intelligent man. The clear message for him here is that his kingdom will ultimately come to an end – it isn't eternal. What questions do you think this might have raised in his mind?

4 Daniel goes on to specifically name the kingdoms that will succeed Nebuchadnezzar's kingdom – the Medo-Persian, Greek and Roman. From our vantage point in history this is awesome, as we can see that the prophecy was fulfilled, which is what makes the dating of Daniel so important. Prophecy can play an import part in convincing people of the truth of Christianity. What is your experience?

5 In the Western world today, we face the secularist marginalisation of religion in general, and of Christian values in particular. Is this true? Can you cite evidence?

6 Secular humanism may be defined as rejection of the supernatural. Can you see how this is happening in our own culture, especially in science, education and other areas of society?

11
When the State Becomes God
Daniel 3

The account of Daniel's three friends in the fiery furnace is one of the most famous Bible stories, and is much loved by those children who are taught it.

Nebuchadnezzar had built a huge golden statue towering above the plain of Dura. His motivation may have been:

- an obsession with the statue with the head of gold from his dream
- simply an opportunity to consolidate his power by getting everyone to bow down to the statue.

Religion and the state

In Daniel 3 Nebuchadnezzar attempts to make his empire and rule absolute by insisting on being treated like a god and worshipped. He attempts to absolutise the relative.

Throughout history humanity has tried to relativise absolutes and instead take relative values and absolutise them. Examples include:

- the state
- power
- wealth
- sex.

When an absolute power like Nebuchadnezzar attempts to prove his invincibility, it is inevitable that others will suffer. What about the fiery furnace episode? Did Daniel's friends suffer? It may be easy to think that because God ultimately rescued them, they did not suffer, but imagine their mental anguish before their rescue.

The price of spiritual integrity

The statue worship appeared initially to Nebuchadnezzar to be a success (Daniel 3:7). But three men did not bow in worship (Daniel 3:8–12). The king was enraged and reacted (Daniel 3:13–15). The three who refused to bow stated their case (Daniel 3:16–18). They considered their lives to be of relative value compared with the absolute value of God.

God had tried to teach Nebuchadnezzar through his dream:

- that his kingdom would be of limited duration
- that his power was limited, not absolute.

Saved in the fire

Nebuchadnezzar was truly astonished. The men had not died, even though those who had cast them into the furnace had. Add to that the appearance of the mysterious fourth figure who was seen in the fire. 'Did we not cast three men bound into the fire?' said Nebuchadnezzar.

'But I see four men unbound, walking in the midst of the fire, and they are not hurt; and the appearance of the fourth is like a son of the gods' (3:24–25).

Nebuchadnezzar discovered that he was not the absolute power in this situation! He had taunted the young men, asking, 'Who was the god who will deliver you out of my hands?' (3:15). Nebuchadnezzar is stunned into praise in Daniel 3:28–30 when he discovers that the young men's God actually will deliver them out of his hands.

There is an important principle here. God is a great deliverer – but we must make our own decisions. So, the young men had to decide for themselves to put God first. After they had done this, God vindicated them.

Nebuchadnezzar was clearly a man of impulsive and volatile extremes. One moment he was raging against God. The next, he was threatening anyone who defamed God.

What about those who follow Jesus? We too are tested. Salvation is a free gift, not earned or deserved, and confession of faith in Christ may cost us everything:

- career
- family
- friends
- even life itself.

And Jesus will enable us to pass the test.

The cost of resisting idolatry is high, but it doesn't compare with the cost of rejecting God.

Application questions

1 The story of Shadrach, Meshach and Abednego is one of the more famous Bible stories. Did you hear the story as a child? How did you react to this story on first hearing it?

2 One of the important lessons of Daniel's prophecy in chapter 3 is that no state is absolute or of unending duration. How did Nebuchadnezzar appear to react to the prophecy?

3 In the prelude to the fiery furnace, Nebuchadnezzar tries to make himself a god to the people of Babylon. He erects a golden image and orders everyone to worship it. Consider the response of the three friends to his order: 'we have no need to answer you in this matter . . . our God whom we serve is able to deliver us from the burning fiery furnace . . . But if not . . . we will not serve your gods or worship the golden image.' What do you think of their response?

4 Nebuchadnezzar's taunt earlier was, 'Who is the god who will deliver you out of my hands?' He found out that there was a God in heaven who could and did exactly that – he delivered the three out of the fiery furnace unscathed. As a result, Nebuchadnezzar praised the God of heaven and ordered the Babylonians to do so as well. Did Nebuchadnezzar learn the lessons God taught him? How will you employ the lessons God is teaching you from this story?

5 The commitment of these young Hebrew men cost them a lot. Just the apprehension the three must have endured as they faced the furnace would have been agonising, yet they bravely faced it knowing that God could deliver them and, even if he didn't, they would not fail him. What about you? Has your faith cost you anything?

6 Look again at Nebuchadnezzar's praise of God in Daniel 3:28–30. If only more people today saw God in the same light. Would you say the three must have had a significant impact on their Babylonian peers? Does God still act in this way? Can you give an example?

12

The Testimony of Nebuchadnezzar

Daniel 4

Chapter 4 of Daniel takes the form of a personal statement about Nebuchadnezzar's experience of God. This text would have been widely read in the ancient world.

Nebuchadnezzar set out the purpose of his testimony: 'It has seemed good to me to show the signs and wonders that the Most High God has done for me' (4:2). His purpose was that the whole of his world would know that God's kingdom existed and was everlasting.

Nebuchadnezzar's polytheism is never far from the surface. Even though he is making this testimony about the one true God, he still refers to Daniel as 'chief of the magicians' and says, 'I know that the spirit of the holy gods is in you.' He is a man on a faith journey still confused by ideas, but wanting to testify to the power of Daniel's God.

Nebuchadnezzar tells how he has had another dream, and asks Daniel to interpret it. This time it is of a splendid majestic tree that is to be cut down. It also tells of a man whose mind is made like that of an animal. Daniel is alarmed to hear this dream.

The nature of true greatness

God's disclosure to Nebuchadnezzar focuses on three colossal things:

- a dream statue
- a golden statue
- a dream tree.

Each of these items says something about how God perceives him. Nebuchadnezzar was a 'big' impressive man in the eyes of his world and was in charge of an empire and its capital city. Babylon enjoyed widespread fame with its hanging gardens, Nebuchadnezzar's bricks, its prosperous citizens.

The depiction of Nebuchadnezzar as a tall and beautiful tree, which provides protection, food and shade, is far from negative. God approves of all these aspects of Nebuchadnezzar and his empire. There may even be parallels with the goodness of the garden of Eden.

God's discipline of Nebuchadnezzar came not because he was a great builder; his fault was in the moral realm. He concentrated on the tree of life, but neglected the tree of good and evil. Nebuchadnezzar's principal character faults were that:

- he had neglected righteousness
- he had shown little mercy to the oppressed
- he was guilty of an overweening pride.

Christianity doesn't say that enjoying beautiful things is wrong. God created us to love beauty and colour, but the proper use of our aesthetic sense should lead to God the creator of beauty. However, if our aesthetic sense becomes our master, it can drive a wedge between us and God. Indeed Adam and Eve were encouraged by the enemy to break free from God and follow their senses. Their temptation was to be like God, knowing good from evil.

In the same way today, we are encouraged to follow our desires and do our own thing. God is perceived by many as the great inhibitor. Our society says that anything is permissible unless it harms someone.

Through Daniel God gave Nebuchadnezzar the opportunity to repent and change his ways, but Nebuchadnezzar failed to take the opportunity. A year after his dream, God's judgement was executed and Nebuchadnezzar fell into some form of insanity.

Human and animal: what's the difference?

The biblical view says that human beings are unique because they are made in the image of God.

- God is spirit.
- Humans are part spirit, part flesh.
- Animals are flesh.

Other views

Peter Singer, a bio-ethicist of Princeton University, describes the biblical view of the superiority of human beings as 'speciesism', which leads to discrimination against or exploitation of animals.[8]

Likewise, John Gray of the London School of Economics says that Christianity's cardinal error is the belief that man is superior to other animals.[9]

A comparison of views

Singer denies:

- that there is a Creator
- that humans are made in the image of God
- the existence of a soul.

The biblical view states:

- humans are made in the image of God
- they are answerable to God as stewards for their attitudes towards animals and their use of the earth.

From intellectual darkness to light

Nebuchadnezzar's punishment is connected with his immense pride. As a result his intellect is darkened and he becomes animal-like. Nebuchadnezzar's case is extreme, but in Romans 1:21–22 Paul warns that rejection of God can lead to 'futile' thinking and 'foolish hearts' that are 'darkened'.

In the Romans passage, the negative Paul mentions is the lack of gratitude to God:

- refusing to acknowledge God by acknowledging indebtedness to him
- refusing to express gratitude to him.

This lack of acknowledgement of God, or potentially in the case of 'New Atheists' downright denial of the existence of God, going as far as to say that religious belief is detrimental to our being, is just as common today.

Otherwise rational people can become irrational:

- suggesting that Jesus did not exist, when the weight of evidence is to the contrary
- offering a 'choice' between God and science, when logic should tell them that theology and science aren't alternatives, but complementary disciplines (God is an explanation in terms of agency, science in terms of mechanism and laws)
- suggesting Christian faith is without evidence and yet refusing to consider evidence when it is provided.

Nebuchadnezzar's downfall was his self-image as originator of Babylon's wonders. As he rejected God's sovereignty he began to die spiritually by descending into darkness, and physically by becoming animal-like.

Some examples from the modern world of art and entertainment apart from God might seem to demonstrate the descent into animal-like behaviour.

Reversing this process of pride requires putting this behaviour into reverse – repentance. It requires a lifting of the heart and mind to God, as Nebuchadnezzar did at the end of this period of darkness. Nebuchadnezzar's confession is clear in Daniel 4:34–37. He is restored to his position, but most importantly he sees that God rules far above him and gives thanks and praise accordingly.

Nebuchadnezzar thought he was above others and Babylon, but he:

- came to see God as he truly is
- bowed his head and heart to honour God
- admitted God was right to humble him.

For Nebuchadnezzar, coming to faith in God brought about a very literal return to reason.

The response to Nebuchadnezzar's testimony

We can only wonder how Nebuchadnezzar's testimony was communicated. Perhaps independently by word of mouth? Or perhaps later on when Daniel wrote his book?

Application questions

1 Nebuchadnezzar's experience of God related in Daniel's book is truly remarkable! Imagine a world leader today who was intent on the whole world knowing that God's kingdom exists and is everlasting. Can you think of any modern-day examples?

2 Who wouldn't have been proud of the city of Babylon, the Babylonian empire and the fame that accompanied these things? But there is a type of pride that gives thanks to God for allowing the accomplishment of great things and there is a pride which assumes sole credit for them. How do we know the king had the latter?

3 The tree of life and the tree of the knowledge of good and evil – the problem of pride goes all the way back to Adam and Eve. Professor Lennox suggests that King Nebuchadnezzar failed in the same way as his progenitors Adam and Eve. Can you see how they wanted to be like God rather than just know God? Is this a problem in our day as well?

4 The discussion leads into a consideration of the difference between humans and animals. It's difficult to believe that people actually make the arguments reported – Peter Singer, John Gray and others. The biblical view is logical and straightforward. What do you think?

5 We are unlikely to have created a vast and beautiful empire like Nebuchadnezzar, but we all have gifts and abilities. What things in your life tempt you to pride? Are you good at remembering where your gifts come from?

6 Paul suggests in 1 Corinthians 13:1–3 that the same can be true of spiritual gifts. Think about the gifts God has given you. Do you exercise them with love? Do you ever see spiritual gifts being used competitively?

13
The Writing on the Wall
Daniel 5

Daniel 5 begins with a new king, Belshazzar. Originally it was thought that Daniel 5 had little or no historical substance as there was no independent record of a king called Belshazzar. This changed with the discovery of the Nabonidus Cylinders in the foundation of a ziggurat in Ur. One of the cylinders named Belshazzar as the son of Nabonidus.

- Nebuchadnezzar died in 562 BC.
- His son, Amel-Marduk (in the Bible, Evil-merodach – see Jeremiah 52:31 and 2 Kings 25:27), reigned 562–560 BC.
- Amel-Marduk was murdered by Mergel Shar-usar, his brother-in-law, who reigned 560–556 BC.
- His son, Labasi-Marduk, reigned for just six months.
- Next came Nabonidus, the last Chaldean (Babylonian) king.

Belshazzar was the son of Nabonidus and co-regent with him during Nabonidus's ten-year absence in Arabia. So he was the second ruler of the kingdom. He was possibly a grandson of Nebuchadnezzar.

A feast fit for a king?

This is one of the most famous episodes of Daniel. We do not know the purpose of the feast, but some have suggested it was to display Babylon's invincibility. We do know, however, that the invitees were a thousand of the lords of Babylon.

Belshazzar called for the Jerusalem Temple vessels that we heard about at the very beginning of Daniel 1. He may have called for them because they were beautiful, and to use them as a display of Babylonian power, or he may have called for them for a much more sinister reason.

Belshazzar knew of Nebuchadnezzar's conversion. He knew about it and yet he rejected it and wanted to show his repudiation of God in a deliberate act of blasphemy. He chose to drink from the Temple vessels, while praising gods of gold, silver, bronze, iron, wood and stone.

The writing on the wall

In an instant, the revelry of the feast and any enjoyment of the blasphemy turned into sheer terror. A mysterious hand began writing on the palace wall. Hastily searching for answers, Belshazzar summoned his advisors, promising great favours to the person who could interpret the writing. However, none of the king's advisors could fathom the inscription.

The appearance of the supernatural hand must have led them to question if there was a realm beyond this one. The words written appeared to be words associated with weights and measures. Was the supernatural hand interested in values? Should they be? The crowd sensed the awesome presence.

Enter the queen (or queen mother?) to investigate. She admonishes the crowd to calm down and refers them to Daniel, who has provided skills of interpretation and wisdom to Nebuchadnezzar in the past. And so, Daniel is summoned to the hall and Belshazzar offers him rich rewards for his knowledge.

Daniel indicts Belshazzar, reminding him of Nebuchadnezzar's experiences (Daniel 5:18–23).

- Nebuchadnezzar knew the source of his success.
- Belshazzar knew about Nebuchadnezzar's search and experiences.
- And yet, Belshazzar publicly defied God by his actions. (What a flagrant breach of the first commandment!)

God's verdict

Daniel's interpretation of the writing and God's verdict is given in Daniel 5:24–28.

- *MENE*: God has numbered the days of your kingdom and brought it to an end.
- *TEKEL*: You have been weighed in the balance and found wanting.
- *PERES*: Your kingdom is divided and given to the Medes and Persians.

God's logic

- Belshazzar's value system was bankrupt.
- Using the holy vessels showed his values.
- Belshazzar's own pleasures and desires were supreme.
- God's desires and pleasure were worthless in Belshazzar's eyes.

Belshazzar's reaction

This is a startling case of divine judgement before death. Belshazzar had been tried and sentenced by God, who had proved beyond doubt that he was his Creator and Judge, and yet Belshazzar continued as if nothing had happened. He rewarded Daniel as he had promised (Daniel 5:29) and made Daniel (Belteshazzar) third in command in the country. Two rulers with very similar names – Belshazzar and Belteshazzar – but opposite fates.

Daniel's history of resisting idolatry brought gain, but the cost of resisting God is incredibly disastrous.

The finger of God

- The hand of God wrote on the wall in Babylon. It would write again in the sand in Jerusalem when Jesus dealt with the woman caught in adultery (John 8:3–11). Unlike Belshazzar, the religious leaders had at least read the writing of God's law, which condemned adultery and demanded that the woman should be stoned. They brought her to Jesus, but he responded in a startling manner.
- He knelt down and wrote with his finger in the sand.
- He responded, 'Let him who is without sin among you be the first to throw a stone at her.'

The woman's accusers probably felt exposed, condemned and ashamed as one by one they walked away.

Jesus responded to the woman, 'Has no one condemned you? . . . Neither do I condemn you; go, and from now on sin no more.'

Jesus Christ had come into the world; he engaged with people in life. He allowed them to see his life, unsullied by sin and unmarked by sinful thought.

It is the same hand that

- wrote the law on stone tablets
- wrote on the walls in Babylon
- wrote on the ground in Jerusalem
- writes on repentant and believing hearts (2 Corinthians 3:3).

God's judgement and our responsibility

Why were Nebuchadnezzar and Belshazzar treated differently? Nebuchadnezzar was disciplined and restored, but Belshazzar perished in the Medo-Persian invasion. Similarly in the New Testament, why was Paul treated differently from Herod?

- Paul persecuted Christians and was let off.
- Herod murdered James and was judged by God.

Paul tells us in 1 Timothy 1:13 that he acted 'ignorantly in unbelief', whereas when Herod was hailed as a god by the people, he 'did not give God the glory' (Acts 12:2, 21–23). These examples show that God's judgements are not arbitrary. Nor could they be, since it would go against the character and the morality of God.

Nebuchadnezzar had had direct personal revelations from God.

Belshazzar knew what had happened to Nebuchadnezzar. He did not act ignorantly. He was responsible for his attitude and behaviour.

Some contemporary atheists, such as A. C. Grayling, say that faith means believing without evidence, but that is not the case. Jesus says, 'Blessed are those who have not seen and yet have believed' (John 20:29). But physically seeing Jesus is not the only kind of evidence we can have. Neglect of God's law is a neglect of evidence.

Blasphemy is not hard to find today. Some atheists actively encourage it. However, we should remember that Belshazzar's blasphemous drinking to idols using the Temple vessels stands in stark contrast to the privilege we Christians have of celebrating the New Covenant.

Application questions

1 Daniel 5 has long been a favourite chapter in the Bible. What has archeology done for this famous story?

2 The writing on the wall has to be one of the scariest stories in history. Imagine a room full of people who have been eating and drinking and enjoying themselves for a couple of hours. Then, out of nowhere, a hand begins to write on the wall. How terrifying would that be? Remember this was long before we had capability to take pictures and project them

on screens or walls. What do you think you would have thought? What would you have done?

3 Belshazzar tries to find someone, anyone, who can explain what is happening. He appeals to the wise men and diviners. Finally, the queen, or more likely the queen mother, Nabonidus's wife, enters the room. She is familiar with Daniel's abilities, so refers the matter to him. Why do you think only she comes up with this idea?

4 MENE, MENE, TEKEL, PARSIN. Why could the king's advisors not translate these words in order to understand the meaning of the writing? Especially the last word, which means 'your kingdom is divided and given to the Medes and Persians'. The Medes were outside the palace at that very moment waiting to conquer mighty Babylon.

5 Professor Lennox sees the common element of 'the finger of God' in the Ten Commandments, the feast in Babylon, and Jesus with the woman of John 8. Would you agree? Why is that?

6 In 2 Corinthians 3:3, Paul writes, 'You are a letter from Christ . . . written . . . on tablets of human hearts.' What has God been writing on your heart recently?

14

The Law of the Medes and Persians

Daniel 6

Daniel 6 introduces us to a new world – the world of Medo-Persian rule. This is the transition from the kingdom of gold to that of silver in Nebuchadnezzar's dream of chapter 2.

Darius the Mede leaves us with a puzzle, as historically we are unable, as yet, to place him. Records are clear that it was Cyrus who took over the kingdom. The only Darius we know of succeeded Cyrus, but archaeological evidence may yet come to light that will help us identify him, as was the case with Belshazzar.

The purpose of the law

The theme of values is a major subject in the first half of Daniel. The theme of laws is prominent in the second half. Laws are based on values, but are not the same as them. Laws uphold values.

The central topic of this chapter is the imposition of law to deny Daniel the right to practise his faith and worship God according to Mosaic Law. This parallels the first chapter of the first half of Daniel, where he refuses to eat the king's food.

The law of God and the laws of the state

Daniel appears to have caught the eye of Darius very early on after his conquest of Babylon. Daniel became 'distinguished above all the other high officials and satraps, because an excellent spirit was in him' (6:3).

He was appointed as one of three who ruled over the 120 satraps (provincial governors), and he was being considered by Darius to have day-to-day control of the entire kingdom. His jealous colleagues in the administration wanted to discredit him but could find no grounds. They decided the only thing of which they could accuse him was his religious belief and practices.

There is great pressure in the Western world today for the privatisation of expression of religious belief. Daniel was prepared to swim 'against the flow'.

Daniel's enemies

Daniel's enemies decided to use his religious convictions against him: they proposed an injunction against religious petitions. They suggested a law that no petitions (prayers) should be allowed for thirty days. Violators would be cast into the lions' den.

Daniel's enemies claimed that:

- this was the unanimous view of officials (clearly Daniel had not been consulted, so this was not true)
- this was for the good and unity of the nation. (It was a move toward the deification of man.)

The proposal, if adopted, would become a law of the Medes and Persians and would therefore be irrevocable, even by the king. It was assumed that Daniel would offend quickly.

Daniel's reaction

When the law was passed, Daniel continued his regular prayers, which for him were a non-negotiable expression of his faith (1 Kings 8:47–50).

Daniel's motivation

Although Daniel lived in Babylon and was faithful in his service to the king, he did not live for Babylon, but for Jerusalem and all it represented. He prayed toward Jerusalem as King Solomon suggested in 1 Kings 8:47–50. As Professor Lennox says, 'The secret of Daniel's life and witness is that he always had a window open towards Jerusalem. He knew that there was a God in heaven who would hear him.'

Daniel's enemies

Daniel's enemies brought charges against Daniel, probably insinuating that he was more loyal to his ethnic origins than to the king – another half-truth. Daniel was true to his God, but he was also loyal to his king.

Darius's response

Darius immediately realised that he had been tricked and was most distressed, trying unsuccessfully to find a loophole that would allow him to spare Daniel.

Government and the rule of law

The law of Babylon was quite different from that of the Medo-Persian empire.

Babylon had been an absolute monarchy. Nebuchadnezzar did whatever he liked, he regarded himself as being above the law. Babylonian culture was not without law. A much earlier king, Hammurabi (1792–1750 BC), had been passionate about justice and the rule of law and had set the country on a good footing.

His code of law was:

- to cause justice to prevail
- to destroy the wicked and evil
- to prevent the strong from oppressing the weak.

Medo-Persia was a constitutional monarchy, which should have been an advance on absolute monarchy, although it was far from the system of democracy later developed in Greece.

The basic human right of equality before the law that is predominant in the West found its origin in Israel, where everyone was subject to the law regardless of status. This goes back to the teaching that we are all made in the image of God.

The Medo-Persian law in question here, the one constructed by jealous officials, contradicted basic morality, discriminating against Daniel and depriving him of what we consider a basic human right.

The Greek legal system which was to come had laws which Aristotle divided into two categories:

- Natural law, which reflects our understanding of who we are and our human nature.
- Positive law, which is determined simply by the will of the ruler.

The law in question here was a positive law and contrary to both natural law and God's law.

In most cases there is no conflict between God's law and natural law. The law of the state usually draws on the other two.

Unfortunately, in this case, once enacted, laws are difficult to reverse. Laws should not be easy to ignore or get around. On this occasion an irreversible law was used as a trap for Daniel. Later, however, the Medo-Persian king, Ahasuerus, used an irreversible law to protect the Jewish people in the time of Queen Esther (Esther 8:8).

A higher law

God's law trumps all human laws. When laws clash, God's law is to be obeyed and in this case God sets the human law at naught. The story of Daniel in the lions' den illustrates the nature of law and its use and abuse.

In many countries today we can observe the increasing use of positive law to discriminate against believers in God.

Application questions

1 Harmonising what Daniel reports about the succession of power in Babylon with what we learn from history has not proved easy. Historians tell us that Cyrus occupied and conquered Babylon in 539 BC. Daniel writes that Darius 'received' the kingdom. What might this unusual wording imply?

2 Daniel saw what was happening in this episode and realised where things were headed, but he was willing to 'swim against the flow'. The ways of the world are often contrary to the ways of the Lord and we need to be willing to go against the flow. Have you ever felt the need to go against the flow? In what ways?

3 The laws of the Medes and Persians being irrevocable is an interesting concept. What do you think about irrevocable laws? Are the laws of your country irrevocable?

4 We have material here on Daniel's motives. Basically, Daniel had only one major goal, which was to live his life in a way that would please the Lord. His sub-goals had to be congruent with his major goal. Have you settled on your major goal? How might we know this about you? Can you think of situations where a sub-goal could clash with your one major goal?

5 What about Daniel's reputation before Darius? Don't you think that if Daniel's enemies had any point of accusation against him whatsoever they would have built their case around that instead of condemning him for his religious practices? Why didn't Darius pick up on this?

6 Aristotle taught the difference between natural law and positive law, but this must have been known or considered for some time before Aristotle formalised it. What do you think about the distinction?

7 The law Darius implemented was contrary to natural law and contrary to God's law. Too bad that Darius hadn't taken one of Aristotle's courses in philosophy! Would things have been different?

15
The Law of the Jungle
Daniel 6

Lion-hunting was a sport of the Mesopotamian kings. The lion was a potent power symbol. Ashurbanipal, who reigned 883–859 BC, apparently killed a total of 450 lions.

Using the lions' den as an execution chamber could have served a dual purpose of eliminating tiresome opponents and keeping the palace lions well fed. But God is sovereign even over lions.

Power politics

Those who reject the supernatural realm of nature will regard the story of Daniel in the lions' den as a myth or legend. However, those who reject the supernatural do so irrationally and unscientifically. Daniel's account deserves to be taken seriously.

Daniel 6 describes a situation of power politics. A group of conspirators used the law to:

- have power over Daniel
- prevent the king from protecting Daniel.

God's power on the other hand:

- restrains the lions from harming Daniel
- does not intervene in the same way for the conspirators when they are thrown to the lions.

So what power does the law have? It has no power in itself – that is why we need law enforcement. Without enforcement, the law is easily ignored.

Lions vs humans

The conspirators plotted to construct a law which would destroy Daniel and prevent the king from protecting him by the agency of lions who survive by instinct (the survival of the fittest) rather than law. The satraps professed to be doing things according to the law. But their law turned quickly into the cruel law of the jungle. Ironically, Daniel's enemies were using the moral law to behave like amoral animals. Daniel had (presumably inadvertently) threatened their territory, so they fought back. In the end, the conspirators suffered the fate that they had planned for Daniel.

The survival of the fittest principle operates widely in society today and is clearly visible in the realms of politics and business. In the first half of the twentieth century it was at the heart of Social Darwinism which spawned eugenics programmes on both sides of the Atlantic. Now, postmodern relativism erodes the concept of truth, morality, and the value of human life. Combined with the cult of the self our egocentric culture defines truth and morality in such a way as to make sure it is 'I' who survives.

Daniel was loyal to his king, but was also prepared to swim against the tide of polytheism, asserting his conviction that there is only one true God – the God of heaven whom he worshipped.

Daniel opened himself to accusations of being

- arrogant
- narrow-minded
- bigoted
- anti-social.

Who did he think he was?!

There are other examples of this through history. For example, during the days of the Roman empire you could worship however you liked, as long as you also worshipped the emperor. The penalty for not doing so was to be thrown into a huge den of lions in an amphitheatre.

Christianity claims to be unique. Jesus said, 'I am the way, and the truth . . .' (John 14:6) enraging those who claim there is no absolute truth.

True tolerance

What does tolerance mean? Tolerance asserts the right to have convictions, to make judgements about right and wrong, and to express those views without fear. It does not demand that we accept the opinions, beliefs and lifestyles of others, although it does demand that we let others live freely. Voltaire's attitude was: 'I disapprove of what you say, but I will defend to the death your right to say it.'

True tolerance is principled.

- It knows how to put up with things and people.
- It knows when to offer criticism.
- It makes judgements without being judgemental.

The new definition of tolerance seems to say that one must never offend by disapproving of another's behaviour or ideas. It disapproves of absolutes, except one: you will be tolerant of everyone else's view. You must be intolerant of intolerance. The danger of such tolerance is that if we are not allowed to make judgements or have convictions, we could descend into an ethical neutrality.

What does this have to do with Daniel and Persia? There is a powerful drive to embed this new form of tolerance into enforceable legislation, just as we see with Daniel.

Taming the tongue

James discusses the problem of our tongues in James 3:7–10. We can successfully tame animals, but struggle to control our own tongues.

The strategy of the satraps in the book of Daniel was to stop Daniel at any price because of their jealousy. They passed a law that would stop Daniel by trapping him. They were destroying him with their tongues in their report.

The obvious extension of this is laws designed to control the tongue and what we say. Some countries today have laws against 'hate speech'. The topic raises questions about whether such laws achieve their objectives, or if they could instead stifle rational moral debate.

We need the resource of the Holy Spirit to not repay evil for evil, but truly to bless others (1 Peter 3:9). Taming the tongue does not mean taking a vow of silence. God's method of communication is his Word (which our lifestyles must back up). We are called to be Christ's witnesses.

We may be afraid of what people will think, but we must share what we know to be true. We will always encounter people who ask questions we have never thought of, and which we can't immediately answer. We should never pretend to have all the answers, but we must always seek to honour Jesus.

Application questions

1 We are seeing a gradual eroding of morality in our times and if we don't wake up and understand what is happening, we may find that it is too late to reverse things. How does this link with the story of Daniel in the lions' den?

2 The first sub-heading in this chapter is 'Power politics', which is defined as using the law to achieve personal goals and ambitions irrespective of the rights of others. Who used power politics in this situation in Daniel 6, and how did they go about it?

3 Animals, especially lions, provide a wonderful illustration of this. Everyone knows and understands the term 'survival of the fittest' and everyone knows why a lion is called 'the king of the jungle'. Animals have no moral code. When people live without regard for moral considerations, how are they acting?

4 'Daniel was clearly prepared to swim against the tide of polytheism and assert his conviction that there is only one true God – the God of heaven whom he worshipped.' What do theism and polytheism have to do with morality and the law?

5 Jesus made the astounding claim, 'I am the way, and the truth, and the life. No one comes to the Father except through me' (John 14:6). Many people think that all religions lead to God and there are simply different ways of getting there. Can this idea be reconciled with Jesus' claim?

6 How can we avoid the logical outcomes of tolerance which John Stuart Mill warns against? ('The tyranny of public opinion that stigmatises and silences minority and dissident beliefs.')

7 As believers we are called to defend the Christian message. This requires using words to explain what the Scriptures mean. We need to do so with kindness and love. Fortunately, logic and common sense make the job easier. Can you share some examples of how you have engaged in this way?

16

The Four Beasts and the Son of Man

Daniel 7

The remainder of the book of Daniel consists of four visions that Daniel himself saw.

- Two occurred in the Babylonian period (606–539 BC).
- Two occurred in the Medo-Persian period (539–330 BC).

Background

See chapter 8 of this guide with regard to the logical structure of Daniel, and the chart on page 226 of *Against the Flow*. The first two visions break the chronological sequence of the narrative.

The four beasts

The first vision involves four wild beasts, which Daniel is told represent four empires. It also refers to the Ancient of Days, the Son of Man, the saints and the future.

Symbolism

The initial part of the vision echoes the creation narrative of Genesis, with the wind and the sea. However, this time it is not a prelude to the formation of a hospitable planet, but to the rise of a sequence of four animals, representing four empires, like Nebuchanezzar's dream. Each empire is bent increasingly on destruction and is increasingly ferocious.

The beasts and the empires they represent

- The lion with eagle's wings is identified with Babylon and Nebuchadnezzar.
- The bear represents the Medo-Persian empire under Darius and Belshazzar.
- The leopard with wings fits well as a symbol for the Greek empire. The leopard's four heads could allude to the fact that after the death of Alexander the Great, the empire was split into four parts.

The Greek empire was split as follows:

- Macedon and Greece under the rule of Cassander
- Syria and Upper Asia under Seleucus
- Asia Minor and Thrace under Lysimachus
- Egypt and Arabia under Ptolemy.

The fourth beast with ten horns, plus another little horn, is not likened to any wild animal. Some think this beast represents the Roman empire.

A glimpse of heaven

In Daniel 7:9, Daniel sees into the very throne room of the universe, where the Ancient of Days takes his seat.

- His clothing is 'white as snow'.
- His hair is 'like pure wool'.

He is resplendent on his throne before an unimaginably large crowd.

- A 'thousand thousands' = 1 million serve him.
- And 'ten thousand times ten thousand' = 100 million stand before him.

The books are opened indicating the court session is ready to begin. But the fourth beast is still speaking 'great words', and insisting on being heard by God. Without further comment the trial is conducted, the sentence executed and the beast is killed. Its body is destroyed by fire. As for the other beasts, their power is removed but their lives are prolonged.

The Son of Man is then presented to the Ancient of Days to be given dominion and honour and a kingdom.

Daniel is disturbed by his vision and wants to know what it means. He is informed that:

- the beasts are four kings who will arise, but
- the saints will receive the kingdom and possess it for ever.

God will not always deliver

Daniel's attention is particularly on the fourth beast with the horns. This beast makes war with the saints and prevails over them. The beast's smallest horn has eyes and 'speaks great things', symbolising human insight and intelligence. However, notably, it lacks a human heart: it is a dreadful, evil, ruthless genius.

Many atrocities have been committed by intelligent people who have held or hold political power, with millions dying at their hands.

This raises the problem of suffering.

- If God can deliver his people, why doesn't he?
- If God can prevent suffering, why doesn't he?

What is the answer to the problem of moral evil? Daniel's vision gives three responses:

- there is to be a judgement
- the Son of Man will come
- the saints will receive the kingdom.

There is to be a judgement

Whatever the details are, it is clear from this passage that brutal, amoral and unjust regimes will not rule for ever.

Some shy away from the idea of judgement – after all, God is a God of love, and talk of judgement can seem medieval and grim. However, far from future judgement being a negative concept, it should be viewed as a cause for joy: suffering, unfairness, discrimination, harassment, persecution and any number of other ills will be justly dealt with by the Ancient of Days when the heavenly court sits.

The Son of Man will come

In Nebuchadnezzar's dream in chapter 2 the magnificent but unstable statue is toppled by a stone that becomes a mighty mountain and eventually fills the whole earth. Here, in chapter 7, the powerful and ferocious beast that tramples everything under foot is destroyed by 'one like a Son of Man'.

There is a powerful message here: the seemingly invincible beasts of power will not reign for ever. A perfect human, the Son of Man, will come to take over from the beasts to rule in perfect justice.

We know who this Son of Man is. Jesus used the title as a description of himself. The Son of Man who is also the Son of God will be the judge of the world. Jesus Christ, who had no personal sin, is alone worthy to assume power. He is the perfect Son of Man – it will be a perfect human who does the judging.

This is the big story that makes sense of history.

- Some 2,600 years ago, Daniel, in a vision, saw the Son of Man coming on the clouds.
- Six centuries later, Jesus told the Jews of the Sanhedrin that they would see him likewise.
- Stephen, at the end of his defence of the gospel before the Sanhedrin, also looked up and saw the Son of Man in the clouds.

The saints will receive the kingdom

The definition of a saint is one who is set apart as sacred or holy. It refers to those who, like Daniel, have set God apart as Lord.

When Jesus is speaking in Matthew 19:28, he says that when the Son of Man sits on his throne, the disciples will also sit on twelve thrones, judging the twelve tribes of Israel. Paul makes it clear that all believers will share in the kingdom and its judgement in 1 Corinthians 6:2.

Some have become atheists because of the problem of evil. And yet, atheism offers no answer to the question of evil. If there is no life to come as atheists suggest, then there is no justice and the saints will never receive the kingdom. There is no explicit mention in Daniel 7 of the resurrection of the dead. However, in Daniel 7:10, 100 million people are described as standing before the throne of God, which suggests this idea. That said, God does reveal a resurrection of the dead to Daniel in 12:2, 13.

John reveals that the great crowd mentioned in Revelation 7:9 are those who have come out of the great tribulation: God has raised them to life. This enormous crowd will watch the judgement of the beast who has eliminated millions: they will see justice done.

- God is sensitive to all injustice.
- God will wipe away all hurt and pain from those who have suffered this tribulation.

A vision of the future

Daniel wanted to know more about the fourth kingdom. In particular, the meaning of:

- the ten horns
- the little horn that spoke great things, and made war with the saints.

Here there are conflicting viewpoints. Some say that we should not concern ourselves with details. Rather, we should be content with general principles. Interpretation of the details of such a prophecy is extremely difficult and can lead to dogmatism and quarrelling. Certainly the general principle is of great value. However, that is not to say that there can't be several levels of fulfilment of a biblical prophecy.

For example, the 'seed' (or 'offspring') of the woman in Genesis 3:15 can variously be interpreted as:

- Eve's seed
- Abraham and Sarah's seed
- King David's seed
- Jesus Christ himself (Galatians 3:16).

Initially come the partial fulfilments of the prophecy, with one final complete fulfilment.

The general principle behind this prophecy is that

- believers will be persecuted by inhuman regimes.

The specifics from Daniel's prophecy are:

- There is a beast with ten horns and a smaller horn that speaks.
- The beast makes war with the saints and prevails.
- The Son of Man comes in the clouds of heaven.
- The heavenly court passes judgement.
- The saints receive the kingdom.

Something similar is described in Revelation 13:1–8.

The beasts described in Daniel 7 and Revelation 13 are very similar, so can we assume that Daniel and John are describing the same thing? What is the reality of which the beast is a symbol? Paul also describes something similar in non-symbolic language in 2 Thessalonians 2:1–10 – the final form of world power that will be destroyed when Christ returns.

This will be a man who sets himself against God. In Revelation this man is given the number 666. Speculation as to what this number represents is pointless. When the time comes there will be no need to guess who this man is.

The fourth beast represents the final manifestation of human rebellion against God. Paul is referring to spiritual lawlessness in 2 Thessalonians. This will be characterised by many leaders who demand to be worshipped, which Daniel himself experienced several times.

An observation: the closer we get to the time of fulfilment, the more detail will be given to us.

A future world government?

This seems to be what Daniel's prophecy implies. Some have suggested that an international world government would indeed be the answer to all the world's problems. Among those who have thought this are:

- Einstein
- Dante
- Kant (with reservations).

Daniel says the final form will be:

- a world government
- of hideous strength
- maximally hostile to God.

So, why should we bother thinking about these things? Paul clearly thought it was vitally important. He warned the Thessalonians about 'the man of lawlessness' and state-orchestrated hostility towards God. In more recent times we have seen this increasing.

The Enlightenment proposed the idea that all true knowledge is value free and objective, and that values are subjective and a matter of taste. Similarly, New Atheist demagogues now announce that science leaves no room for God, and that faith in him has no evidential basis.

Daniel, however, shows where the elimination of God will lead. Not to freedom, but to incalculable oppression. Earlier, we saw that some people hope the kingdom of God on earth will come as Christian teaching permeates society, so that government structures will become Christian.

The biblical 'map' of Daniel 2 and 7 says the opposite: the kingdom of God will arrive with the return of Christ to oppose the beast and his kingdom.

Preparing for the future

There are two words of warning about this prophecy:

- Some details will only be understood at the time of their fulfilment.
- We need to take it seriously but avoid speculation.

There are two reactions from Daniel:

- Jesus will return and execute justice.

- He was rightly greatly disturbed by the prophecies.

Professor Lennox concludes:

- Jesus, risen from the dead, is the key to hope.
- Faith is thoroughly evidence-based.
- The appropriate response to the evil embedded in government structures is engagement, not withdrawal; Daniel and Paul are examples (2 Thessalonians 2:7).
- We should be salt and light in society!

Application questions

1 The chart on page 226 of *Against the Flow* is very helpful in understanding this chapter. As you read through the chart you can't help but appreciate the cosmic nature and importance of the visions Daniel is describing to us. Was this a new way of looking at things for you? How so?

2 The first and second beasts are clearly Babylon and Medo-Persia in both of which kingdoms Daniel actually lived. We expect to read history in the Bible and we expect that it will be accurately portrayed. What do you think? Did Daniel pass the test as a chronicler of the historical events of his times?

3 The third and fourth beasts – Greece and the ten-horned beast – are future to Daniel. So his insights here are truly prophetic. What is your reaction to reading prophecy in Scripture? What do you know about the history of Greece? Did Daniel get it right? We don't really know much about the ten-horned beast – some think it was the Roman empire, others that it concerns the future. Are you OK to accept some ambiguity here? Could the idea of partial fulfilment and final fulfilment be appropriate here?

4 'There came one like a son of man, and he came to the Ancient of Days and was presented before him' (7:13). Even we can figure out who these figures are. The first is Jesus and the second is God. How do you feel when you read that one like a son of man is coming and that Jesus will eventually return to set things right?

5 There will be a judgement. This is one of the clear conclusions of Daniel 7 and Daniel sees this as a good thing. It should also be easy for us to conclude that it is a good thing. If there is no judgement, evil people get away with evil deeds and that is a bad thing. What examples can you think of to illustrate the point?

6 Daniel eventually pronounces that, despite the fact that the fourth beast will prevail over them, the saints will ultimately receive the kingdom. What will this look like? How do we know that they won't lose it again? Can you cite a reference?

7 At the end of this vision, Daniel shares his reaction with us: 'my thoughts greatly alarmed me . . .' These things should greatly alarm us too and we must continually remind ourselves that one day Jesus will come and set everything right. Until then we must be engaged in pursuing truth and what is right. Are you? How?

17

The Vision of the Ram and the Goat

Daniel 8

This vision in Daniel 8 concerns two animals:

- a ram, representing the Medo-Persian empire
- a goat, representing the Greek empire.

If we are correct in identifying the four animals in chapter 7 as the four empires of chapter 2 – Babylon, Medo-Persia, Greece and Rome – then this means that chapter 8 concerns itself with the middle two of these empires.

At the time of the vision, Daniel was in Susa (now in modern Iran), the capital of Persia. He found himself beside the Ulai river (canal). The vision took place during Belshazzar's reign.

The vision described

The ram had two horns and was incredibly powerful. No other animal could stand in its way or rescue anything from it. It did exactly as it pleased.

The goat suddenly appeared from the west. It had one prominent horn between its eyes. It gored the ram and trampled it. Its power was unparalleled for a time. Then its horn broke and was replaced by four other horns.

A further horn grows from one of these four. It increases to a huge size and challenges heaven, casting angels and stars to the ground. It ends the regular burnt offering and desecrates the sanctuary. Daniel then hears a conversation between holy beings, asking how long the desecration will last. The sanctuary will be restored after 2,300 evenings and mornings.

The vision explained

The vision is explained to Daniel by 'one having the appearance of a man' called Gabriel. Gabriel explains that the ram is Medo-Persia, the goat is Greece.

From our position in history we are able to identify the large horn as Alexander the Great, who died in 323 BC. Following his death, his empire was divided into four parts, each represented by the four horns:

- Cassander ruled Macedonia and Greece
- Lysimachus ruled Thrace and Asia Minor
- Seleucus ruled northern Syria and Mesopotamia
- Ptolemy ruled southern Syria, Palestine and Egypt.

The little horn represents Antiochus IV who gained control of Israel and committed horrible atrocities against the Jews.

Daniel's role explained

He was not a historian reporting his experiences. He was a prophet with a vision from God. From his first vision he had learned that the fourth beast would:

- change the times
- change the law

in order to overcome the people of God.

Now he is told that the little horn will also defy God and his law, like the fourth beast of chapter 7.

A pattern emerges, describing deteriorating attitudes towards God and his law by pagan kings.

The future and beyond

Gabriel tells Daniel that this vision is 'for the time of the end'. How is this so? Just as we looked at partial and complete fulfilment of prophecy in the previous chapter, Antiochus is a shadow of things to come. Another leader like Antiochus will arise.

The prophecies of Daniel chapters 2, 7 and 8 (and, as we shall see, 9 and 11) all focus on this final government that will be destroyed by the coming of Christ. The different prophecies give us different perspectives on the same events, similar to the way in which the four Gospels give us different perspectives on the same events.

The prophecies also link conceptually to the ideas of 2 Thessalonians 1–10.

The spread of Greek culture

One of the legacies of Alexander's conquests was that Greek culture spread over a vast area. Alexander's death signifies the beginning of the Hellenistic Age from 323 to 30 BC. The period between 280 and 160 BC produced many thinkers who would lay the foundations for science as we know it:

- Euclid in the field of mathematics
- Aristarchus of Samos – astronomy
- Archimedes – mathematics
- Eratosthenes of Cyrene – geography and mathematics (also astronomy, music theory, poetry and athletics)
- Hipparchus – observational astronomy
- Polybius – a historian whose ideas on the separation of powers in government ultimately influenced the drafting of the Constitution of the United States of America
- Dionysius Thrax – Greek grammar.

Alexandria was named after Alexander the Great and was a leading research centre with its famous library. Callimachus, a leading Greek poet of the third century BC, catalogued an estimated 500,000 scrolls that had been housed there.

Greek law formed the basis of economic and political activity. Accepting Hellenistic culture became advantageous to local populations, and so Greek religion became pervasive, with temples being built as far east as Iran.

The Seleucid kingdom

Antioch in Syria was the capital of the kingdom, and it was from here that Antiochus IV came. The kingdom covered a vast and unwieldy area including Asia Minor, Mesopotamia and Iran. Many factions across this large area led to weak government. The Greek empire was ultimately annexed by the Roman empire. Antiochus IV's father, Antiochus III, was defeated by the Romans in 191 BC at the battle of Thermopylae and forced to give up territory. In 198 BC he defeated the Egyptians in Panium and so brought Ptolemaic rule in Judea to an end. Initially, he gave the Jews a degree of autonomy, although he began a programme of Hellenisation, to include placing idols in the Temple. The Jewish people protested and he backed down. Antiochus IV took the throne in 175 BC and proved to be a very different ruler.

Antiochus Epiphanes

Antiochus chose the title 'Epiphanes' to express the belief that he was 'God manifest'. In order to consolidate power across his culturally diverse empire he drove forward the process of Hellenisation and one religion for all. This, of course, came into conflict with what he saw as the narrow-minded exclusivism of Judaism, which demanded devotion to one God and the rejection of all others.

Antiochus Epiphanes encouraged the Mediterranean people to worship him as the Canaanite god, Baal. As is recorded in the apocryphal book of 1 Maccabees, some Jewish people found the Greek culture attractive. It made fewer moral demands on them than Judaism and allowed freedom of their impulses and desires, as well as opening up new avenues of entertainment and sport. It promoted the free exchange of ideas minus religion. This new 'freedom' was enjoyed by even the Jewish high priest Jason in this regard.

On this there is a similarity to current views, where people make similar choices to abandon God, because they think he is out to stifle people and their self-expression. People want freedom from any authority above humankind. The Greek ideal in life was the pursuit of happiness, in which human beings were the measure of all things. Just as some of the Jews of Antiochus's era bought into a watered-down version of their faith, Christians of our times can buy into a watered-down version of their faith.[10] Orthodox Jews believed in a God of revelation, which was beyond the comprehension of Greeks, as it can also be for many modern people.

The challenge before Antiochus

The centre of gravity for Jews was their God. Their loyalty transcended loyalty to any king. And their first commandment was to have no other gods. Antiochus tried to change their loyalty. He deliberately desecrated their Temple by removing:

- the golden altar
- the golden lampstand
- many gold and silver vessels.

These items are not enumerated in Daniel's vision, but we are brought back to the beginning of Daniel's story, when Nebuchadnezzar looted vessels from the Temple.

Antiochus commanded his subjects to forsake their customs and follow those 'strange to the land', as is recorded in the book of 1 Maccabees, in which we are also told that all the Gentiles and 'many even from Israel'

- sacrificed to idols
- sacrificed pigs and other unclean animals
- neglected circumcision.

Antiochus forbade Sabbath observances and, as Daniel had seen, stopped the daily sacrifice. He held pagan sacrifices on the altar instead, which was an utter abomination to the Jews. Determined to break the spirit of the people, he banned the reading of the law of Moses and ordered that all copies should be collected and burned. He banned the observance of the law on penalty of death even going to the extent of murdering Jewish babies who had been circumcised. His ultimate act of blasphemy was to rededicate the Temple to Zeus. This was the final 'abomination'.

What was the response?

Unlike some of the immediate responses of God seen earlier in the book of Daniel, he appears to do nothing. How could a pagan defy the living God, abolish his commandments, reverse his ordinances and get away with it? However, Antiochus failed to reckon with the depth of anger he had provoked, in what we now call the Maccabean Revolt, led by Judas Maccabeus. Judas Maccabeus formed a resistance group against Seleucid occupation, determined to reverse the evils that Antiochus had imposed on them. Eventually, all of Jerusalem was recaptured except for Antiochus's citadel. The Temple was cleansed and new priests chosen. Eventually, they rededicated the Temple to God, which is celebrated to this day by way of the festival of Hanukkah.

God made manifest

Almost two centuries later, Jesus is in Jerusalem in the Temple precincts at Hanukkah. John records (10:22–33) that the Jews ask him if he is the Christ. His response is, 'I and the Father are one.' Jesus stands where Antiochus Epiphanes ('God made manifest') had stood. Was history repeating itself? His accusers decided that he had blasphemed, and picked up stones to stone him.

Jesus tells them that their rejection of him as their king will mean another period of exile and further destruction of their city. He refers in Matthew 24:15–30 to Daniel's prophecy of the abomination of desolation as something yet to happen.

'So when you see the abomination of desolation spoken of by the prophet

Daniel, standing in the holy place (let the reader understand), then let those who are in Judea flee to the mountains . . . For then there will be great tribulation . . . .'
(verses 15–16, 21)

So, in the future, another man will stand where Antiochus blasphemed against God and where Jesus made his valid claim to be God. We learn that:

- this man will reject the supernatural God
- his faith will be in himself alone
- he will use human emotion to enhance his position and power
- he will be supremely intelligent
- he will possess unparalleled power.

But his dominion will come to an end. Daniel predicts that after 2,300 days the sanctuary will be restored. Jesus confirms that he will return in power and glory to destroy the man of lawlessness and usher in his kingdom.

The end of Antiochus's time

Antiochus died in the year of the rededication of the Temple. Judas Maccabeus maintained a peace of sorts, but died five years later to be succeeded by his brother, Jonathan. Jonathan became a friend of the new king, Alexander Belas, who made him High Priest, thus starting the Hasmonian dynasty. However, Jonathan was not descended from Aaron, as the law of Moses stipulated a high priest should be. This alienated those who adhered to the traditional way of thinking and who formed a powerful opposition, later to be known as the Pharisees. Jonathan was assassinated and replaced by his brother, Simon. Simon was assassinated and replaced by his son, John Hyrcanus I. John Hyrcanus was a Sadducee at heart and as such denied the supernatural and embraced materialism.

Anti-God ideologies will continue

History is not yet over and Daniel's warning still stands. The events of Antiochus's time will repeat themselves in a different form in the future, but on a greater scale. We live in the calm before the storm. Until recently Western culture has been a more or less Christian culture, enabling life to flourish. However, there has been and continues to be huge amounts of bloodshed. Stalin, Mao, Pol Pot and Hitler killed millions. If we replace state-enforced pagan culture of Seleucid times with state atheism of more modern times, the motives that drove Antiochus are still very much alive. Enver Hoxha of

Albania, for example, in 1976, stated in the Constitution that every form of religion was to be banned and atheistic propaganda would be supported instead 'in order to implant a scientific materialistic world outlook in people' (Article 37).

The state ideology of North Korea, *Juche,* is a political ideology with pseudo-religious characteristics, built on the deification and mystification of Kim Il-sung. Those unwilling to accept the belief system are considered traitors and are legally punishable. It is an ideology imposed on the population through fear and terror – a prime example of totalitarianism.

Totalitarianism employs deceit and manipulation of people to keep them from perceiving the truth. Just like the little horn of Daniel 8:12, 'it will throw truth to the ground'. In 2 Thessalonians 2:9, Paul speaks of the coming of the man of lawlessness in similar terms. The relation of power to truth is very important. Postmodern relativism means that people are interested in their own feelings, or what works for them, rather than in the question of what is actually true. This weakens resistance to totalitarianism.

Why should we take Daniel's vision seriously? Violence is not dying out. Aggressive atheism is increasing at the intellectual and propagandist level. In secularised Western societies, there is pressure to marginalise religious belief. Nations are increasingly discriminating against believers.

What, then, is the solution? Paul identifies the source of evil:

- we have inherited a fallen nature
- we have all individually sinned.

The role of Enlightenment thinking is a blind spot in Western perception. We need to embrace Daniel's God-given vision.

Application questions

1 The 'time of the end' is something which has captured the attention of thinking people throughout history. People like Daniel, and John with his Revelation, describe for us, with God's enabling, what it will be like as the world as we know it comes to an end. Is this information helpful? How so?

2 The spread of Greek culture that took place throughout the Mediterranean world and subsequently Europe is astounding. Galatians 4:4 uses the term 'when the fullness of time had come' to allude to perfect timing. The time was certainly right for Greek culture to engulf the region. People were ready for new ways of looking at things. What evidence does Professor Lennox give us here?

3 Antiochus Epiphanes was a powerful character. We are told that 'Epiphanes' means 'God made manifest'. What utter arrogance for a man, even a significant one like Antiochus, to claim that he is God in human flesh! Aren't you grateful that God is not like Antiochus? Antiochus always thought of himself; God thinks of others. Are there any other differences you noted?

4 Antiochus really initiated a systematic programme for Hellenising the Jewish people. What are some of the things he did? Can you understand why he was uniformly hated by the Jews? Was his effort effective?

5 People both in Daniel's time and today have a wrong view of God, which causes them to abandon or turn their backs on him. Many think of God as a sort of cosmic spoilsport. That is, he makes us do the things we don't want to do, and he prevents us from doing the things we really want to do. Can you explain why this view of God is mistaken?

6 Jesus made the claim in the Temple, 'I and the Father are one' (John 10:24–33). What is the difference between Jesus claiming to be God manifest and Antiochus claiming the same thing?

7 We end this chapter with the question, 'Why should we take Daniel seriously?' This is a question for which we need to have a good answer. When we blow prophecy away, we don't have a good answer, do we? How would you answer the question?

18
Jerusalem and the Future
Daniel 9

Daniel's final visions both concern writings:

1 from Jeremiah the prophet
2 'a book of truth' from an angelic messenger.

Both visions are dated to the time of the Medo-Persian empire. In the first we are in the times of Darius the Mede, who was tricked into passing a law to forbid prayer. Daniel prays nevertheless, with his window open towards Jerusalem.

It seems that Daniel's heart is always concerned with Jerusalem – the centre of Jewish worship. Daniel lived in Babylon, but he lived *for* Jerusalem. He prayed regularly and he also studied the Scriptures. On this occasion he has been reading Jeremiah's prophecy about the amount of time to be spent under Babylon's rule (Jeremiah 25:8–12). Daniel responds to this word with prayer and fasting (Daniel 9:2–3).

Praying with the Scriptures

Daniel's reaction to Jeremiah's words shows that he believed the Scriptures were the word of God. Daniel knew that the seventy years under the rule of Babylon were almost over. He may have wondered what he could do towards the restoration of Jerusalem. We do know that he set himself to seek God's wisdom and guidance. Daniel believed that God could speak both through the Scriptures (as he did through the passage in Jeremiah) and directly (as through Daniel's visions).

Daniel is very interested in the way God authenticates his existence. In Daniel 9 he does this by self-authentication through his word. 'All Scripture is breathed out by God,' says 2 Timothy 3:16.

The external evidence for this is based on

- history
- manuscripts
- archaeology
- science.

Professor Lennox explains his own early experience of seeking God through his word: not merely seeking knowledge about God, but seeking God himself.

Daniel too waited on God until he heard and saw him. Daniel's prayer in chapter 9 is a great confession on behalf of his people about his beloved home, and stands in deep contrast to Nebuchadnezzar's pride in Babylon in chapter 4. He makes no excuses for the people's rejection of God through their behaviour. He acknowledges that God has warned them about the consequences of their actions, and he sees that as a result a devastating calamity has overtaken them. They should have known it would happen, since Moses himself has told the people long ago about the promises of blessing if they kept God's commands, and what would happen if they did not. But Leviticus 26:40–45 offers a ray of hope if they confess and humble themselves before God.

Daniel seizes on that promise and pleads with sincerity on behalf of his nation. He seeks God's mercy.

Daniel cares not only for Jerusalem but also God's reputation.

God answers Daniel's prayer

Daniel receives a dramatic answer to his prayer, with a visit from Gabriel. Gabriel had visited Daniel earlier in the vision in chapter 8. Gabriel addresses Daniel by name and tells him he has a message for him because he is greatly loved.

We read of Gabriel in connection with three people in the Bible: Daniel to whom he appears twice; Zechariah, the father of John the Baptist in Luke 1:11, 19; and Mary in Luke 1:30–33. Gabriel's visits involve prophecies about major supernatural interventions in history:

- to Daniel about the time of the end
- to Zechariah about the coming of the last and greatest prophet, John the Baptist
- to Mary, bringing the ultimate response to Daniel's prayer – Jesus!

Jesus himself showed immense concern for Jerusalem and its people, and it would be wrong to think that this is restricted to Old Testament times.

- Jesus wept as he announced to the city the consequences of its rejection of him as the Messiah (Luke 19:41).
- Jesus predicted its downfall and the destruction of Herod's Temple by the Romans (Luke 21).
- Jesus warned of desolations and exile for the nation leading far into the future (Luke 21:23–27).

Just as Daniel viewed the time of the end through the lens of the terrible deeds of Antiochus Epiphanes, Jesus viewed the end time through the lens of the destruction of the Temple. The disciples associated the destruction of the Temple with Christ's return.

Jesus cites the fulfilment of one of Daniel's predictions as a key event in the future: the abomination of desolation. There are three references to it in Daniel (9:27, 11:31 and 12:11).

Application questions

1 Throughout all of the intrigue in the kingdoms and amidst his own personal struggles, Daniel is always focused on what will happen to Jerusalem. Why is this so?

2 Daniel is assured that in the end the saints will receive the kingdom. In Daniel's time this was not certain given the events of the times. What do Jesus and the New Testament writers have to say about this?

3 The statement 'Daniel lived in Babylon, but he lived *for* Jerusalem' is profound. Would you like something similar said about you? Is there anything you need to do so that you and everyone else are clear on what you are living for?

4 When Daniel realised the calamity facing his nation and his people, what was his response?

5 Daniel's prayer in Daniel 9 can only be described as awesome! Reread the prayer. Have you ever prayed like this?

6 It is interesting to think of the way we view the time of the end based on our place in the history of the world. Daniel viewed it from the times of Antiochus Epiphanes, Jesus from the times of the Roman empire and the disciples from the destruction of the Temple. What is our perspective?

19
The Seventy Weeks
Daniel 9

What is unique to Daniel chapter 9 that we do not see in chapters 2, 7 and 8? The answer is the prophecy of the seventy weeks.

There is much controversy and disagreement, even among experts, on the interpretation of the seventy weeks referred to in this chapter.

Some useful considerations

The seventy weeks are represented as the sum of seven weeks, sixty-two weeks and one week. 'Week' is a translation for the Hebrew word 'seven', but what does it refer to? Some think these weeks are symbolic and not tied to any chronology. Many others think that a week represents seven years – so the total period is 490 years.

When do the seventy weeks begin? Daniel talks about the edict to restore Jerusalem in Daniel 9:25. Several such edicts are mentioned in the Bible. Ezra 1 talks of Cyrus's decree authorising exiles to return and to rebuild the Temple. Artaxerxes subsequently halts the rebuilding of the Temple until further notice (Ezra 4:21), and it is not rebuilt until Nehemiah puts in his bold request to Artaxerxes in the twentieth year of his reign. Some consider this as the starting point of the seventy weeks.

Putting the prophetic background together

Daniel's prophecy in Daniel 9:24–26 speaks of sixty-two weeks, plus seven weeks. Jeremiah's prophecy in Jeremiah 25:1–12 and Jeremiah 29:10 also speaks of seventy years.

Commands to rebuild the Temple/Jerusalem come in:

- 538 BC from Cyrus to rebuild the Temple (Ezra 1:2–4) (this becomes known as Zerubbabel's Temple)
- 521 BC from Darius to rebuild the Temple (Ezra 6:1–10)

- 457 BC from Ezra to finish the Temple (Ezra 7:1–27)
- 445 BC from Artaxerxes to rebuild Jerusalem (Nehemiah 2:1–8).

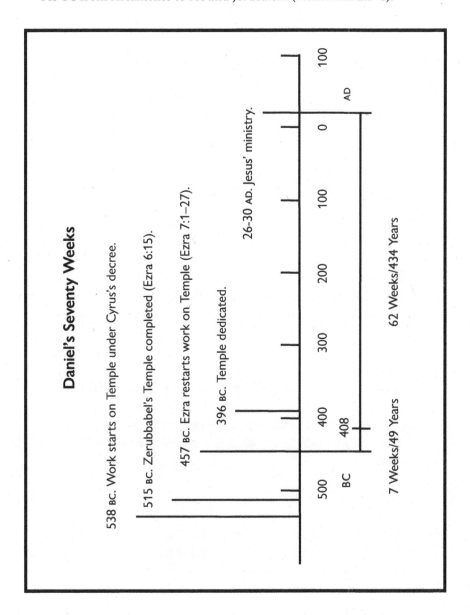

Daniel's Seventy Weeks

538 BC. Work starts on Temple under Cyrus's decree.

515 BC. Zerubbabel's Temple completed (Ezra 6:15).

457 BC. Ezra restarts work on Temple (Ezra 7:1–27).

396 BC. Temple dedicated.

26–30 AD. Jesus' ministry.

7 Weeks/49 Years

62 Weeks/434 Years

BC   AD

500   400   300   200   100   0   100

408

Which calendar?

Whichever calendar you use – the Gregorian one that is in use today, or the lunar one, which was in use in Daniel's day – with appropriate corrections, both yield the same result. Thus, Daniel's prediction of when the Messiah, Jesus, would be cut off (crucified) was phenomenally accurate.

What about the seventieth week?

We will address the seventieth week in the next chapter. We don't want to let disagreement on that score detract from the accuracy of Daniel's prophecy.

Application questions

1 Daniel's prophecy of seventy weeks is not without controversy. There are different ways of interpreting it. We have chosen one of these for our analysis of the prophecy and people may well disagree with us. We would suggest that the weeks represent years, so 490 years from the beginning of work on Ezra's Temple until the time the Messiah would be 'cut off', with one week in the future remaining. What is your view of this approach?

2 The prophecies of Jeremiah and Daniel are nothing short of astounding. As we have commented, the areas of prophecy and archaeology, the manuscript evidence, and the agreement of the Bible with what we know from science offer powerful evidence that the Bible is reliable. What do you think?

3 One of the puzzling things in the mystery before us has to do with the difference between Zerubbabel's Temple and Ezra's Temple. Can you explain the problem and the facts?

20
The Seventieth Week
Daniel 9

Two interpretations

- The 'traditional view' is that the seventieth week immediately follows the sixty-ninth.
- The second view holds that the seventieth week is still in the future – even to us today.

Some considerations

The traditional view is that the seventy weeks (of years) are consecutive – this is easier to visualise. However, the seven years following Jesus' death in AD 30 do not match the description in Daniel. By moving the start date of the seventy weeks forward, we can include the destruction of Jerusalem by the armies of Titus, but many of the other details seem to fit, including the offer of the covenant of Daniel 9:26–27.

It is arguable that there is internal evidence in Daniel 9 that supports the view that the final week does not follow on directly from the previous sixty-nine. Jesus' teaching also seems to support this view when he speaks of:

- the destruction of Jerusalem followed by wars and rumours of wars (Matthew 26:4)
- Jerusalem being trampled by Gentiles (Luke 21:24)
- 'the abomination of desolation' before Christ's return (Matthew 24:15).

The book of Revelation seems to corroborate this view as it refers to a period of time when the holy city will be trampled underfoot (Revelation 11:2).

The teaching of the apostles also seems to support this view:

- Paul's teaching at the Areopagus on Jesus' return (Acts 17:31).
- Peter's teaching on the new heavens and new earth (2 Peter 3:1–13).

We may ask why we should worry about one small period of seven years. However, it is God's response to Daniel's concern for Jerusalem; God was assuring Daniel of future restoration and that Gentile domination would end. See Romans 9:2–3 for Paul's similar concerns.

Implications for dating the book

As David Gooding (1981) demonstrates, the structure of Daniel argues for an early date with the deliberate placing of chapter 9 to parallel chapter 4.

- Chapter 4 describes the success of Nebuchadnezzar: he sins, but is restored by God.
- Chapter 9 compares God's discipline of Nebuchadnezzar with God's discipline of Jerusalem, which also will be restored.

In chapter 4:

- no blame is assigned to the Babylonian culture
- no blame is accorded to Nebuchadnezzar
- all blame is laid on Israel's persistence in sin.

The fate of Antiochus argues against parallelism. Unlike Nebuchadnezzar he does not repent and continues unchanged to the end, when he meets a violent death. The book of Daniel was not written to encourage the Jews that God would treat Antiochus as he did Nebuchadnezzar.

Application questions

1 In this chapter we have two interpretations of the seventieth week. Can you explain them? We tend to prefer simple things. Unfortunately, the simple explanation here is probably not the best. Can you explain why?

2 Some scholars think these are adequate reasons for ruling out the traditional view of the seventieth week. What do you think?

3 Scholars suggest that internal evidence from Daniel supports the future view of the seventieth week. What is this? Can you suggest some internal evidence from the book of Daniel that argues for the future view?

4 The teaching of Jesus seems to be the clincher. Summarise his points in this regard.

5 The question 'Why bother with one week?' is a good one and the answer is powerful. It shows God's great love and concern for those who work for him, doesn't it? Was this section encouraging for you?

6 Earlier, we saw that the book of Daniel is dated by many scholars to 605–550 BC. Some scholars, though, date the book to the second century BC. Why is this even important? What does it matter?

7 What do you think of the arguments David Gooding presents for the early dating of the book? Did they convince you? Could you use them to argue the case for an early date for Daniel?

21
The Man above the River
Daniel 10

Daniel 10–12 reveals the fourth vision God gave Daniel. Daniel dates it to the third year of Cyrus and locates it on the banks of the Tigris river. The vision describes the coming of a great conflict.

A brief sketch of the vision

Daniel sees a glorious figure above the river. He is overwhelmed and falls asleep. He is awakened by a heavenly messenger who will cause Daniel to understand what will happen to the Jewish people in the future. The messenger has been delayed by unseen powers but reveals what is written in the book.

The messenger gives a lengthy historical survey which:

- begins in Daniel's time in Medo-Persia
- traces the rise of the Greek empire under Alexander
- details the division of that empire into four parts
- describes the conflict between the various parts of the empire.

The conflicts are between:

- the kings of the north (Seleucids)
- the kings of the south (Ptolemies).

This culminates in the desecration of the Temple by Antiochus IV 'Epiphanes'.

The messenger uses the time of Antiochus as a prototype, when a fierce king will:

- arise and exalt himself
- magnify himself above every god
- cause terrible trouble for Daniel's people.

Daniel is told to seal the book until the end.

Daniel then sees two figures on opposite banks of the river. He hears a question directed to the man above the river, 'How long shall it be until the end of these wonders?' (12:6). He hears the answer: 'time, times, and half a time' (12:7). He doesn't understand the answer so he asks for clarification. However, he is told that the words are sealed.

At the end of the vision he is given a beautiful promise (Daniel 12:12).

A message from heaven

Daniel is told that what he sees is inscribed in the book of truth (10:21). His previous vision was received while he was reading another 'book of truth': the book of Jeremiah.

Some conclude that if the book of truth contains detailed revelations about a time in the future, we can't take it seriously. If it were true it would lead to a deterministic (semi-deistic) view of God, in which God has wound everything up like a clock. It would allow no room for human responsibility if certain events have been predicted in writing. It could suggest that whoever is behind the prediction causes the events to happen, and that there is no freedom of decision or action. However, this would only arguably be the case if God's relationship to time is the same as ours.

Daniel dates the vision to the third year of the reign of Cyrus. Daniel would have been in his eighties by this time, when the Jews were allowed by Cyrus to return to Jerusalem to rebuild the Temple. It seems that Daniel did not go with them. This is strong evidence for Daniel's book having been written early rather than later. It is argued that if the events were written in the second century, a neater fictional ending would have been for Daniel to return to his beloved Jerusalem.

Daniel receives the vision

From the tone of the book of Ezra, we can surmise that Daniel would have been deeply concerned about the reports coming from Jerusalem. In fact, he describes himself as being in a time of 'mourning', during which he eats very little. This both echoes and contrasts with his refusal to eat unclean food on his arrival in Babylon. In the first instance, he didn't eat to avoid compromising himself; this second time he is not eating out of concern for his nation. Daniel is still resolute in his faith. Is he fasting in the hope of hearing more from God?

The flow of history

Daniel is by the waters of the Tigris as he receives the vision. Rivers had already been used by Jewish writers as a poetic metaphor expressing the flow of history.

As he stands there, he becomes aware of a man *above* the river. The man's appearance is described and it becomes clear that this is no mere human or even an angel. This figure is overwhelmingly transcendent in his glory. The way that Daniel describes him is mirrored in John's description of his vision of the risen ascended Christ. Daniel's unnamed companions don't see the vision, but they do sense that something profound is happening and run and hide.

The impact of the vision on Daniel is such that his strength ebbs away and he collapses to the ground and falls into a deep sleep (just as John does, when he sees the risen ascended Christ – see John 20). The next thing he knows, he is trembling on his hands and knees and hears a voice telling him not to fear. A supernatural messenger tells Daniel that he is greatly loved by God. Far from being rejected by his questioning, Daniel is affirmed by the love of God. Twenty-six centuries on, we can hear the same message from God himself, incarnate in his Son (John 3:16).

The words of the messenger to Daniel reveal Daniel's attitude at the beginning of his time of fasting – and indeed heaven's attitude to Daniel. Daniel has humbled himself before God, his questioning has been heard and a messenger has been sent to respond to him immediately. The messenger is delayed by the prince of the kingdom of Persia but is eventually able to reach Daniel.

A messenger from heaven

The fact that the heavenly messenger was hindered seems an extraordinary statement, and opens a window into an unseen realm of supernatural beings – of angels and demons. So, who are the angels? The Bible tells us that they are 'ministering spirits sent out to serve for the sake of those who are to inherit salvation' (Hebrews 1:14). Humans who are made of both spirit and flesh are described also in Hebrews as 'a little lower than the angels' (2:7 NIV).

The messenger reveals that a battle is raging in another world that in some senses reflects the conflicts in this world. This idea recurs in the book of Revelation (12:7-9). Cosmic conflict is not a peripheral notion of Christian extremists. Paul clearly tells us that there are spiritual forces arrayed against us, which we need to take seriously and deflect with the full armour of God (Ephesians 6:10-12).

When Daniel hears that the angel has come to tell him what will happen to the Jewish nation in the latter days, he is once again struck dumb. The supernatural being once again touches and strengthens him and tells him again that he is greatly loved. In Daniel 10:21 – 11:1 the messenger (whom we may assume to be Gabriel) reveals that he was aided by another prince, Michael, 'who has charge of your people' (12:1).

Daniel was being reassured that there is a mighty prince in a higher realm guarding his people.

Application questions

1 In this chapter we read about the fourth vision God gave to Daniel. The main character in the vision is described in Daniel 10:4–6 (and 12:7). Who do you think he is?

2 The vision presents a lengthy historical survey, beginning in Daniel's time in Medo-Persia and progressing through the Greek empire under Alexander the Great, the Seleucids and Ptolemies, ending with Antiochus IV 'Epiphanes'. What do you think are the most important points about these kingdoms in relation to the book of Daniel?

3 Daniel dates the vision to the third year of the reign of Cyrus (536 BC). This is two years after Cyrus permitted the Jews to return to Jerusalem (538 BC). Why do we spend time trying to determine the dates of biblical events? Are they important to our study of Daniel?

4 The message from heaven informs us that a battle is raging in another world and it mirrors what is happening in this world when spiritual forces are aligned against us. What do you think of these forces and their impact?

22
The Book of Truth
Daniel 11

'And now I will show you the truth,' says Daniel 11:2. This is a claim of supernatural truth, not the forecast of clever wise men. The content of Daniel 11 leads us back to the question of whether Daniel is a book of prophecy, or whether it is history disguised as prophecy. Daniel's writing fits so well with history that some claim it must have been written after the fact. The angelic messenger tells Daniel that the vision is for 'days yet to come' (Daniel 10:14).

The phrase 'the time of the end' occurs in 11:40 and in 12:4. However, by common consent Daniel 11:21–25 describes the time of Antiochus. It seems that perhaps it is used here and in chapter 8 as a prototype of what will happen in the end times.

A prototype of the end time

The problem with using an event in history as a prototype is that people will inevitably confuse the prototype with the main event. Daniel had to be very clear on this point: the time of Antiochus would not be the end time, although some may have thought it was. Lord Sacks, former Chief Rabbi of the UK, in his analysis of why religion goes wrong, writes that 'people attempt to bring about the end of time in the midst of time'.[11]

There is a parallel in the New Testament when Jesus used the fall of Jerusalem as a prototype of the end of time, but warned his disciples to be careful not to confuse it, or other events, with the end of time (Luke 21:8–9). As examples of attempting to bring the end of time within time, Lord Sacks cites the two major rebellions against Rome in AD 66 and AD 132, which led to the destruction of the Temple and city and resulted in 58,000 deaths.

Daniel 11 is not a prophetic list to be checked against subsequent historical events in order to confirm our faith, even though it does perform that role. It was also written to warn people of Daniel's time – and beyond – of the danger of misreading signs of the times and concluding erroneously that the end times has come.

The general structure of Daniel 11

Daniel divides the future into four periods:

- **Period 1 (11:5–19).** The messenger warns Daniel that in this period, when Antiochus III occupies Israel, violent Jews will rebel in fulfilment of the vision, but will fail.
- **Period 2 (11:20–28).** This covers the time when Antiochus IV and Ptolemy V of Egypt scheme, but the angel points out that their plans will come to nothing 'for the end is yet to be at the time appointed' (11:27).
- **Period 3 (11:29–35).** Antiochus IV will violently impose Greek culture upon the Jewish people and incite the Maccabean uprising; eventually the Temple will be won back and rededicated, but the persecutions will continue until the time of the end.
- **Period 4 (11:36 – 12:3).** There are many who think that all of Daniel 11 and 12 concerns only the time of Antiochus. However, if this were so Antiochus would have returned to make another attack on Egypt (11:40); he would have had great success (11:43); but he would have been killed while returning (11:45); there would have been a time of trouble for Israel, but eventually the Jewish people would have been delivered (12:1); this in turn would have led to the resurrection of the dead (12:2) at the end of time.

Daniel is told that the timescale for this will be 'for a time, times, and half a time' (12:7). He is also told that roughly three-and-a-half years will elapse after the regular burnt offering is taken away and the abomination of desolation is set up in the Temple area of Jerusalem (12:11).

If Daniel was written after the fact, all of the 'predictions' would have occurred (11:40 – 12:12), but none of them had. Daniel predicted the rise of a fourth empire, Rome, thus the time of Antiochus was not the end.

Predictive prophecy

Is there such a thing as predictive prophecy? The answer determines which world-view is true. Is it biblical theism with its supernatural dimension, or naturalism which denies the possibility of miracles? Professor Lennox has shown that there is strong evidence that this is not *vaticinium ex eventu* (history disguised as prophecy).

Looking beyond Antiochus

It has been possible to identify historical events up to Daniel 11:35 by using extra-biblical sources.

After this the task becomes more difficult.

Is Daniel still referring to Antiochus in Daniel 11:36–39? He was certainly wilful and prideful and exalted himself. He was anti-God, like the new atheists, but he promoted the Greek gods. And there are some other problematic statements:

- 'He shall prosper' (11:36) – did not happen.
- 'He shall pay no attention to the gods of his fathers' (11:37) – Livy contradicts this, as does Polybius.

These statements make it difficult to see Antiochus as the 'king of the north'.

The events of Daniel 11:40–45 cannot be identified in history, because they have not happened yet; they are still in the future. So, as in Daniel 8, we come back to the idea of Antiochus as a prototype. An altogether more sinister leader will appear and he will exalt himself as God. The transition between Periods 3 and 4 shows Antiochus as king of the north blending into the end-time king of the north: the man of lawlessness and the beast from the sea. Theodotian and Hippolytus thought that the transition from Antichocus to end-time king happened in Daniel 11:36, whereas Jerome thought it happened in Daniel 11:21, with a few historical allusions occurring later.

Application questions

1 The big issue we face in chapter 11 is whether we believe its content is true predictive prophecy or history masquerading as prophecy. Did God actually reveal to Daniel what would happen in the future or did Daniel write of events which had already happened and pass them off as prophecy? What do you think?

2 We are introduced to the concept of prototypes – examples used to illustrate various things – which can be useful. We are also told that prototypes can be problematic. In chapter 11, the question is when does the time of the end come? Is it during the lifetime of Antiochus or is it later? Has it come or do we have to look beyond Antiochus the prototype? What do you think?

3 The book of Daniel covers four historical periods. However, when we begin to consider Period 4, we have to be very careful. Why is this?

4 One answer for why Daniel chapter 11 is so loaded with details which actually came to pass in history is that Daniel simply reported on events that were divinely revealed to him through predictive prophecy. Why might people disagree with this view?

23

The Time of the End

Daniel 12

As we begin this final chapter of the book of Daniel, we need to remember that the fulfilment of biblical prophecy is usually much more involved than we might imagine.

What we are able to understand from Daniel is that there are three periods leading up to the time of the end and that the end of time will not occur during the time of the Greek empire, but much later.

Approaching Armageddon

Here are some of the broad contours we discern from Daniel concerning the time of the end.

The future end-time leader is not Antiochus, but another who will:

- invade Egypt and the land of Israel
- take Egypt's wealth and invade a wider region of North Africa
- eventually leave the region alarmed by threats from the east and the north
- meet his end on his way to tackle those threats.

John, in the book of Revelation, speaks of:

- the gathering of kings at the battle of Armageddon (Revelation 16:14, 16)
- the final battle against the kings and the beast (Revelation 19:19)
- the rider on the white horse descending from heaven who conquers (Revelation 19:11).

Paul also mentions these events in 2 Thessalonians 2:8.

This end-time scenario is often met with derision, not only because it is supernatural, but also because some hold that human beings will make such moral progress that aggression and war will become unthinkable. However, the evidence of the last century would seem to contradict this idea. But according to Daniel 12:1, the worst of times is yet to come. Jesus says the same in Matthew 24:15–31. The context of the tribulation varies depending on the speaker's view of the times. Jesus places it in the context of his return and the gathering of the elect. Daniel places it in the context of deliverance for the Jews and the resurrection.

Names written in the book

Daniel describes the worst of times and the best of times. For those whose names are written in the book, there will be resurrection of the body from the dead to everlasting life. However, there is another side: some will awake to shame and eternal contempt. Humans have been given freedom of choice in a moral universe, but this carries with it responsibility and accountability. We have seen in Daniel 7 that God will judge the world when the Son of Man returns, but one's name must be found written in the book.

Revelation 20:12, 15 describes something similar to Daniel 7, where books are opened and the dead are judged by what is written in the books. Revelation 21:27 describes the process. Having one's name written in 'the Lamb's book of life' is essential for entry into God's heavenly kingdom. John explains in his Gospel that in order to enter God's kingdom, you must be born again (John 3:3), and that new life is gained by trusting Jesus Christ (20:31). It is whether or not one has trusted Christ for salvation that will determine the verdict at the final judgement, rather than any 'works' one might have done. This is the principle of faith.

How does this sit with the statement in Revelation 20:12 that 'the dead were judged . . . according to what they had done'? Is this contradictory?

Lennox makes the point that in courts of law there is a distinction between the *verdict* (guilty or not guilty) and the *sentence*. Two people may be found guilty of murder, but their sentences may be different, according to whether there are any mitigating circumstances.

- Matthew 11:20–24 shows that people have rejected Jesus, despite having witnessed his mighty works. Here, Jesus indicates that the sentence will vary according to opportunity and privilege.
- In 1 Corinthians 3:10–15 Paul is concerned to show that behaviour does matter.

So, the condition for salvation is not merit but faith in Christ, and Christ as Judge has the final word:

- John 3:16–18
- John 3:19.

We should note that since the verdict will turn on whether a person has trusted

Christ or not, it follows logically and morally that he or she must have been capable of doing so.

Some deduce from Revelation 13:8 that long before the earth existed God put the names of the saved in the book of life. However, this clearly stands in contradiction to what has been suggested above. The idea of names being written in a book is first seen in Exodus. In Exodus 32:30–33 the idea of 'blotting' names out of the book is put forward. So, it seems from this and Revelation 3:5 that names can be removed from the book due to sin against God.

However, we are assured that faith in Jesus as Son of God enables us to overcome and never have our names blotted out of the book of life (1 John 5:5).

Rising from the sleep of death

The resurrection that Daniel speaks of here resembles that described in 1 Corinthians 15:20–24. It is a resurrection that validates the lives and works of the faithful (1 Corinthians 15:58; Daniel 12:3).

How long?

As the vision draws to a close, 'someone', possibly Daniel himself, asks the figure in linen above the river the burning question: 'How long shall it be till the end of these wonders?' (Daniel 12:6). Daniel hears the answer but doesn't understand. He is informed that one day he will, but 'the words are shut up and sealed until the time of the end' (12:9). Daniel is assured that 'you shall rest and you shall stand in your allotted place at the end of the days' (12:13). We too can be sure of our allotted place if we have put our trust in Jesus, the Son of Man, the Son of God (John 14:1–6).

Application questions

1 All of the things we have seen in Daniel are nothing short of astonishing. But as remarkable as it is, it can only take us so far. There is much still to happen before the end, and we cannot know these things unless God chooses to reveal them to us. What is left to know?

2 Daniel gives us some broad contours about the rest of time: rulers, battles, the final battle. Who is the beast about whom we are told? Is this useful information to know? What should we do about it?

3 The academic community struggles with talk of resurrection because it goes against the view that material is everything. The result of resurrection is that mind (information) is primary, and matter is secondary. Can you explain this?

4 Think about the idea that resurrection of the body, from the dead to everlasting life, is the only answer to human longing. What is human longing? Has the notion of resurrection satisfied your own personal longing? How?

5 The condition for eternal life according to Scripture is not deeds or works but belief. One of the best-known passages of the Bible supports this idea – John 3:16–18. Read the verses on page 348 of *Against the Flow* and make sure that you understand what Scripture says on this point. Do you agree with it?

6 A choice statement of Lennox that deserves mention is 'For those who trust Christ, one of the practical implications of his resurrection is that it gives their life and work for him a wonderful, ultimate validation.' Can you explain how this has been true in your experience?

List of Sources

Butterfield, Herbert, *Christianity and History*, London, G. Bell & Sons, 1949; Collins: Fontana, 1957, 1964.

Costas, Orlando E., *Christ Outside the Gate*, Maryknoll, New York, Orbis Books, 1982.

Dawkins, Richard, *A Devil's Chaplain*, London, Weidenfeld and Nicholson, 2003.

Frankl, Viktor, *Man's Search for Meaning*, New York, Simon and Schuster Pocket Books, 1985.

Gray, John, *Straw Dogs*, London, Granta Publications, 2003, p. 37.

Newbigin, Lesslie, *The Gospel in a Pluralist Society*, London, SPCK, 1989.

Ratzinger, Joseph, Homily, Vatican Basilica, 18 April 2005.

Peter Singer, "Sanctity of Life or Quality of Life?", *Paediatrics* Vol. 72, No.1, July 1983, pp. 128–29.

Sacks, Jonathan, *The Great Partnership: God, Science and the Search for Meaning*, London, Hodder and Stoughton, 2011.

Notes

1 Newbigin, Lesslie, *The Gospel in a Pluralist Society*, London, SPCK, 1989, p. 71.

2 Butterfield, Herbert, *Christianity and History*, London, G. Bell & Sons, 1949; Collins: Fontana, 1957, 1964, p. 147.

3 Dawkins, Richard, *A Devil's Chaplain*, London, Weidenfeld and Nicholson, 2003, p. 248.

4 Frankl, Viktor, *Man's Search for Meaning*, New York, Simon and Schuster Pocket Books, 1985.

5 Joseph Ratzinger, Homily, Vatican Basilica, 18 April 2005.

6 Butterfield, Herbert, *Christianity and History*, London, G. Bell & Sons, 1949; Collins: Fontana, 1957, 1964, p. 82.

7 Protagoras.

8 Peter Singer, "Sanctity of Life or Quality of Life?", *Paediatrics* Vol. 72, No.1, July 1983, pp. 128–29.

9 Gray, John, *Straw Dogs*, London, Granta Publications, 2003, p. 37.

10 Costas, Orlando E., *Christ Outside the Gate*, Maryknoll, New York, Orbis Books, 1982.

11 Sacks, Jonathan, *The Great Partnership: God, Science and the Search for Meaning*, London, Hodder and Stoughton, 2011, p. 5.